PRAISE FOR *T.*
OF DAR

CW00820455

"Sensitive and with an eye to guiding others who are seeking psychedelic medicine, James W. Jesso highlights the tutorial nature of the psilocybin experience, showing how psilocybin mushrooms can be used as a therapeutic tool to face, and subsequently integrate, buried psychological traumas. A courageous and valuable addition to the growing field of psilocybinetics!"

— Simon G. Powell, *Author of The Psilocybin Solution and Magic Mushroom Explorer*

"Behind every great theory there lies a great story, and James' adventures and learning curves with the Psilocybe mushroom is no exception. The True Light of Darkness is an engaging and entertaining tale of the author's bemushroomed ways, and deserves to be picked and tried by the curious and the psychonauts alike."

— Robert Dickins, *Editorial Director for Psychedelic Press UK*

"James has written three cautionary tales of high-dose mushroom experiences, each one focused on reaching for the light by going through the darkness. His ability to re-create the journey in compelling detail, combined with his own observations made during and later while integrating the insights is accurate, savvy and sensitive. He directly confronts his deepest demons: self-loathing and being unable to love with courage, candor and even a sense of humor. A welcome addition to the mapping of consciousness."

— James Fadiman, Ph.D., *Microdose Researcher and Author of The Psychedelic Explorer's Guide: Safe, Therapeutic and Sacred Journeys*

"*The True Light of Darkness* is a journey into a place of feeling, understanding, knowledge and inner strength. It is a brave expose of uncovering the veils and depths of being, when our egos are confronted with questions of who we are. The book looks at Psilocybe medicine in the true context of its ability to fragment and integrate. It is a noble contribution to the fungal pharmacy."

— Robert Rogers, *Clinical Herbalist and Author of*
The Fungal Pharmacy

"*The True Light of Darkness* is James W. Jesso's latest foray into documenting not just his own psilocybin explorations, but in laying down maps of consciousness for those that come after. Jesso bravely recounts three engaging journeys across the emotional, physical and psychic spectrum to reveal the healing power these entheogenic substances have in disentangling the mind, freeing repressed emotion and erasing societal conditioning. There are some witty, insightful and downright hilarious moments in Jesso's journeys, and collectively they enrich the cultural tapestry not just as trip reports, but as reflections of the eternal mystery. Jesso gives language to the highs and lows, the mystical intuitions and the transmissions from within, but he crafts the delivery in an everyman style that you can relate to, and you will certainly want to read."

— Rak Razam, *Writer and Producer of Aya:Awakenings*

"Part psychological thriller, part meditation on the transform-ative potential of psychedelics, at heart this book is a spiritual autobiography revealing Jesso's quest for healing, integration and forgiveness. It's beautifully written. You don't have to be a psychonaut or even a mushroom lover to enjoy and deeply appreciate this book. I suspect Jesso has other rabbit holes to explore and we'll all benefit from whatever he finds."

— Richard Meech, *Director of Ayahuasca:Vine Of The Soul*

The True Light of Darkness

DISCLAIMER

This book is intended as an informational guide for educational and philosophical purposes. Neither the author nor the publisher encourage, endorse, or support illegal or dangerous behavior of any kind. Readers assume full responsibility for their choices and actions, including but not limited to, any physical, psychological, or social consequences resulting from the ingestion of psychedelic substances or their derivatives.

Apart from special exceptions for Joshua Walker and Skye Dreamer, both of whom offered me verbal permission to use their real names, the names of those featured in these stories have been altered to protect their identity.

The True Light of Darkness

James W. Jesso

SOULSLANTERN

Copyright © 2015 by James Jesso
SoulsLantern Publishing
Calgary, Alberta

THE TRUE LIGHT OF DARKNESS

All rights reserved.
No part of this book, except for brief review, may be reproduced, stored in a retrieval system, or transmitted in any form or by any means--electronic, mechanical, photocopying, or otherwise--without written permission of the author directly.
Contact: **contact@jameswjesso.com**

Cover Design - Shannon Reinholdt
Interior Design - Kyle Flemmer
Editing Support - Robyn Roopchan

Library and Archives Canada Cataloguing in Publication Data
Jesso, James W., 1986-, author
    The true light of darkness / James W. Jesso
    Issued in print and electronic formats:
    ISBN 978-0-9919435-8-6 (pbk.)
    ISBN 978-0-9919435-9-3 (electronic)
    1. Psilocybin. 2. Mushrooms, Hallucinogenic. I. Title.
    BF209.H36J483   2015
    C2015-900419-5   C2015-900420-9

To everyone who is living to create a new paradigm for entheogens in the modern world.

CONTENTS

FORWARD

Given the deeply personal, storytelling nature of this book, as well as the underlying intention behind its words, I feel it best to start this foreword with the origin story of my friendship with James and his influence in my life.

I first met James while attending a mutual friend's fundraiser event at a community hall in my home city of Calgary, Canada. I was managing a table for an organization I had helped build called Evolver Calgary with my fellow co-founder and long-time friend, Josh. Another friend had recommended that we attend James' presentation that day, so we left our table duties and ventured forth to see what he was all about. I forget what the topic of that particular presentation was, but I remember sitting in a cozy room full of tiny hard chairs that reminded me of being in elementary school and listening in rapture to the passionate man speaking at the front. Josh, sitting next to me, was equally blown away, and it was clear to both of us that we needed James to come and speak at an Evolver event.

That simple request to present at an event, reminiscent of the innocent request of one child to another upon first meeting in the park and asking, "Will you be my friend?" sparked a colourfully interwoven tapestry of friendship and collaboration through the space and time of the following years. I knew that day I had met someone who would be a powerful inspiration in my life and an agent of change for the world. James continues to show me a level of devotion to his gifts that I rarely come across.

His equally dedicated efforts to share his gifts in service to the wellbeing and evolution of the planet make it easy for me to support his message and story.

When I read James' first book, *Decomposing the Shadow: Lessons From the Psilocybin Mushroom*, I shared a desire I know was shared by the many others who also read it. We wanted to hear James' personal stories, his life experience. Responding in true servant leadership style, James wrote this present text, which gives personal context to his evolving relationship with the psilocybin mushroom.

The True Light of Darkness uses the written word to take readers through the author's many layers of being, brought about with the ingestion of psilocybin mushrooms, and integrated through story. This book is an intimate examination of three incredibly vulnerable experiences and serves as a map for the alchemization of painful wounds into the light of the gift contained within. It exposes a depth of self that requires courage to share in such transparency, and for that, I am grateful that someone such as James is willing to take this step for the collective healing of the planet.

Cultures across the Earth and throughout history have cultivated the use of various plant medicines to maintain a harmonious relationship with the planet, each other, and the self. Western culture's repression and denial of such plants has left most of the population disconnected from a deeper sense of what we might call *Spirit*; a recognition of the interconnectedness of all that exists; that we are each a part of something larger than our individual selves.

In my personal experiences working with plant medicines, it is very clear that these teachers serve the purpose of awakening such interconnected awareness within individuals, often by exposing our raw, naked, and common *humanness* underneath the layers of cultural indoctrination. Since I see this awakening as a foundational element to the shift required to carry humanity across the crises we are faced with today, I am inspired by James' dedication to creating discourse around the use of the "magic" psilocybin mushroom. His writing cracks open the societal eggshell of taboo that surrounds the use of this ancient medicine. James recognizes the value of the mushroom and other entheogens in our world and strives to make available a balanced perspective of the beneficial gifts of individual psychospiritual maturation they offer.

Life is a ceremony. These four words have stuck with me since my first time in the jungles of Peru, and are exemplified by *The True Light of Darkness*. The experiential map that James provides for navigating the psilocybin mushroom experience extends to any of life's challenges and opens readers up to the transformative power of observation, trust, and acceptance. We cannot reach the light without first traversing the darkness. The tools to do this for one's self are artfully communicated through the stories expressed in the following pages. I hope you enjoy diving into *The True Light of Darkness* as much as I did, and may its words ripple out into the world and serve to awaken humanity to their interconnectedness with, as James puts it, *The All That Is, All At Once*.

— Skye Dreamer, *Author of The Spirit of the Gift: A Storymap of Living in the Gift*

AUTHOR'S NOTE

The stories that you will read in this book are about my experiences with a family of powerful psychoactive fungi, the psilocybin mushrooms. Many people have taken these mushrooms, and many more talk of them. Within the conversation, however, there is often a blank spot when it comes to the truly dark experiences. I have written extensively about hard and uncomfortable experiences being beneficial to one's psychospiritual maturation; however, those are not the 'really dark experiences'. The really dark ones are the ones that come out of mistakes being made in the set, setting, and dose, when things go wrong. They are the stories that most people try to forget. Yet, within these stories are great lessons. Not only of the grandiose epiphanies of transformation and healing psychedelics can offer, but about how to avoid repeating the mistakes that brought us to such unnecessary darkness in the first place.

The latter two stories in this book are particularly dark, and I want it to be clearly stated that much of the challenges that came with them were a direct result of the manner in which I chose to situate those experiences. The places I took myself with the mushroom in these stories are psychologically dangerous places, places one need not go to in order to obtain benefit. Places I would prefer never to go again and places I would never suggest another to attempt exploring. Not all of my experiences were like this; many were beautiful, albeit not always comfortable. And these really dark experiences aren't necessarily bad, or valueless.

I am grateful for that darkness I have faced and the fortitude it has offered me, though I also hope to never recreate this type of experience for myself, if I can avoid it. I was lucky to make it out the other ends of these sessions without long-term psychological damage. Others might not be so lucky.

I want it to be very clear that though this book is written partially for the play of reading and storytelling, it is also a serious cautionary tale. There is rising volume to the talk of psilocybin as a tool for psychotherapy and alleviating depression. Along with psychedelic culture's romanticism with experiences like the 'heroic dose', the chances of someone with a psychiatric disorder reaching out for this medicine and getting hurt rather than health is high. The cautionary elements of this book are to expose how dark, painful and potentially damaging these experiences can be when they lack certain support structures, such as a guide, a supportive community and an understanding of one's psychology. It also offers how I managed my way through them as what can hopefully be a life-raft for those who may find themselves as lost in the throes of the psychedelic experience gone dark.

There are many comments made in this book about depression, and I speak with the authority to my own experience. However, I have no 'formal training' and thus my reading and perspectives are limited. The comments made about the nature of depression are not to be taken as a doctrine and I please ask anyone facing depression not to take my words as the complete truth. These comments are only my experience, please do not to take my words as the complete truth. There is so much more to depression than any of us fully understand, and if you are facing it, please see someone who knows more than me. Or at the very least, don't make any rash decisions, such as eating a psychedelic substance, without a lot of research and the support of a loved one or professional.

I offer the same suggestion to anyone with a history of psychiatric disorders in themselves or their family. Even when psychedelics are taken in all the right contexts, though seldom, they may still trigger long-term activation of these disorders.

This book is written to be educative entertainment, but the deepest intension is greater health, understanding and wisdom for all of us through sharing stories and welcoming conversation. I hope that in exploring this, you find not only the insights I intended to communicate, but also the ones buried so deep in the story that I still have yet to fully understand.

Please, be careful with your choices.

Thank you.

ACKNOWLEDGEMENTS

It takes a tribe to raise a book.

Since the release of *Decomposing The Shadow: Lessons From the Psilocybin Mushroom* (2013), I have been continuously encouraged to write this book. The first and most vital acknowledgement is to all the people who supported me in my journey with *Decomposing The Shadow*. Most self-published books amount to very little and thanks to, that one changed my life for the better.

On an intellectual level, I have a deep gratitude to the work of Neal Goldsmith, Stanislav Grof, Martin W. Ball, Joseph Campbell, Baba Ram Doss, Jiddu Krishnamurti, and Stephen Harrod Buhner, among others, for the models of the mind that have so positively influence my writing.

This book, like *Decomposing The Shadow*, wouldn't exist without the generous funding of the larger entheogenic community. So a huge thanks to everyone who donated to the campaign and helped bring this book into material reality. A special thanks to Wes Pryor, whose donation went above and beyond what a normal human should be offering towards a humble book project. Also, a big thanks to Eduardo Khen Mainero, James Williston, Joshua Walker, Simon Haiduk, and Andrew Pawley for producing original artwork for the Indiegogo campaign.

In regards to the production of the book, there were a small handful of people who helped bring this together. Most importantly, Robyn Roopchan who stuck it out with me as my editor over the last year and a half. She has been a blessing to this book and it wouldn't be nearly as good without her. Furthermore, it wouldn't look as cool without Shannon Reignholdt designing the cover. She took a lot of care and attention to craft something original, inspired and emergent out of very ambiguous suggestions from me. She's a hero. Another thanks to Eduardo Khen Mainero for designing the website through his company *Eyenod Studios* and Kyle Flemmer of *The Blasted Tree* for designing the interior of the book.

The promotion of this book was deeply supported by a handful of established authors in the entheogenic culture who wrote reviews, promotional blurbs, and generally stood behind the project. These people include Robert Rogers, Rak Razam, Daniel Micheli, Michael Garfield, James Fadiman, Richard Meech, and Simon Powell. With a special thanks to Skye Dreamer for not only writing a promo blurb, but also the foreword.

On a personal level, I would like to thank my friends and family for their constant support. If it weren't for the people who truly know and love me offering their expressed acknowledgement of my value and the belief in me, I likely wouldn't have the confidence to keep trying. They know who they are and so no names are needed here.

Lastly, I would like to thank You. If it weren't for the important role you are about to play as the reader, this book would be nothing more than a series of abstract shapes. It is you who will bring it to life.

INTRODUCTION

As the resurgence of psychedelic drug use in the Western world takes its firm footing at the base of the underground, a new psychedelic culture is sprouting forth into the mainstream. The premise of psychedelics as tools for personal transformation and spiritual development, as well as for assisting clinical psychotherapy, is finding its foundation in the contemporary cultural ethos. With this fresh spike in popularity comes experimentation of all sorts; a double-edged sword.

Psychedelics have the potential to free us from neurotic patterns, mental illness, defunct belief systems, and address deep-seated emotional traumas successfully. However, they also have the potential to worsen these very issues. The mutability of the experience they offer is highly influenced by set, setting, and dose. Set is the mindset, or everything one brings to the experience emotionally and psychologically, including the fundamental paradigm by which they view the substance itself; setting is the physical location of the experience; and dose is the choice of substance and amount taken. Most recently, it has become more recognized that a fourth element, integration, the application of the insights garnered from the psychedelic experience into one's daily life and basic identity, also plays a powerful role.

These elements are commonly recognized as important factors to consider within therapeutic psychedelic research, but not always understood and successfully applied within their use amongst the cultural underground. This is a vitally important issue to address, as the rising popularity of psychedelic use warrants the necessity of accurate and balanced information regarding their use to be proliferated through to the cultures experimenting with them. To do this, we need to work together to transform the cultural rhetoric surrounding psychedelics to be inspired by the constantly developing and updated human knowledge base on their potential, influencing the common 'set' by which they are engaged. This will help to not only lessen detrimental side effects of psychedelics within this cultural usage, but also accentuate their benefits.

When I began studying and writing on psychedelics about five years ago, the common rhetoric surrounding psychedelics within the underground culture experimenting with them as tools for personal growth seemed to lack direct influence by advances in scientific research (from both academic and citizen scientists) or information from elders (e.g., seasoned psychonauts and career researchers on the subject). Rather, it seemed as though it was directed most readily by the merger of commonly held belief systems within new age spirituality and electronic dance music culture. This is not necessarily a bad thing, as life is an opportunity to creatively render a multitude of interesting realities for ourselves, but I perceived it as a limitation.

In order to fully advance to new levels of understanding and apply the potential of psychedelic use within contemporary human society, it is important that we create a rhetoric, a set, founded on the updated human knowledge base as a whole. It is important that we build integral models for navigating the psychedelic experience that are easy to communicate and understand. Having such models available will help further enable healthy and effective integration of psychedelic experiences, which will in turn feed back into the grander rhetoric surrounding them as well.

I attempted to create such a model for the experience of 'magic' psilocybin mushrooms in my book *Decomposing The Shadow*.

Based on my own practice and successful convalescence from post-drug abuse depression and psychosis, *Decomposing The Shadow* presents a complete cognitive and conceptual model for the psilocybin experience as it relates to psychospiritual maturation and the repatterning of past emotional trauma. I discussed the history, science, spiritual practice, and psychology of the experience and explored a full picture of what the experience may show us about the nature of human emotion and how it plays out in mental health, in the person, and in society. The greatest focus was on the dark experiences of psychedelics and how they can be navigated to be of great spiritual and personal benefit, as I perceive them as being amongst the most valuable, yet the least discussed. I also offered suggestions on setting the stage for one's journey, as well as navigating and integrating the experience. This was done with the intention to offer an objective framework and rhetoric for navigating and integrating the psilocybin experience effectively towards personal development: self-guided psychedelic psychotherapy.

I was blown away as a self-published independent author for this book to be so well received and for its popularity to take me touring all across Canada in the summer of its release, sharing its message with others, transforming the cultural rhetoric through discourse and community. I received a lot of positive feedback and was honoured to hear how *Decomposing The Shadow* has positively affected so many people.

The cultural situation around psychedelics is transforming radically at this time, and what I perceived as a situation of unhealthy religiosity within psychedelic is softening. That being said, the journey towards the co-creation of integral models for navigating the psychedelic experience is forever ongoing. One of the specific areas where these models are still lacking is the effective navigation of the dark experiences, especially without religious connotations. These are often the experiences we most readily want to forget. Yet, the integration of such experiences is key to the life lessons psychedelics have to offer us.

In an effort to further our potential for integrating the dark experiences psilocybin can offer and expand the model introduced in my first book, I offer you *The True Light Of Darkness*.

As *Decomposing The Shadow* was a book presented to engage the intellect, a book established on an accessibly scholarly approach to the psychology of psilocybin-educed spiritual experiences, its demographic is limited to a certain subset of people. Within the pages of this book, I offer a storytelling narrative to engage the heart and hopefully offer my process of effectively navigating deeply challenging emotional experiences with psychedelics to an even broader audience.

The three stories in this book explore three different calibres of the psilocybin experience as they manifested in my personal consciousness, how I navigated and integrated them, as well as the explanations of the psychological, social, and spiritual mechanisms they expose. Established in the conceptual framework of *Decomposing The Shadow*, I offer you, with as much honesty as I could muster, three of my most notable experiences of facing the darkness of my psyche through psilocybin. Each story takes place at different points of development within my own practice, and they progress with increasing darkness and complexity.

2 Friends, 5 Dried Grams, and a Box from Cusco, Peru takes place just before I finished my first draft manuscript of *Decomposing The Shadow*, over a year before its release. It begins in the daytime with two friends before progressing into contextually significant but comparatively minimal personal challenges. It is on the lighter end of psychedelic potential, as the intention between us was simply to share and explore a mushroom experience. *The True Light of Darkness* occurs in the winter of 2012, just before the culturally aggrandized winter equinox of December 21st. This story recounts a night with one friend that was initiated with the intention to face personal malaise and sadness. Its insights are complex and its darkness is psychotic. *Embracing The Shadow; Facing Forgiveness* takes place about two months before the launch of *Decomposing The Shadow* and was written after my summer tour. It starts with the intention to face one of the most intense bouts of depression I have ever experienced, on a high dose, in a sensory isolation float tank. It ends with having progressed through a set of emotions and thought patterns that remain amongst the most terrifying and painful psilocybin experiences I have ever had, at an intensity I hope to never face again.

I have placed great care and attention to fill this book with the valuable insights and perspectives earned in my committed practice with psilocybin, yet its real value will not be of my doing. It will be of yours.

The Story is a vessel of consciousness, and through participation as observers, we can isolate, discover, and inter-connect insights beyond the storyteller. One taps their deep consciousness in storytelling, and through the 'vehicle' of language offers far more than the storyteller is able to recognize on their own. So the real value of a book comes from the 'meaningfulness' and insights unlocked by you, the reader, in relationship to the story and through the vehicle of your experience.

I consider the content in these pages as being filled with hard-earned and valuable knowledge, presented in a way that will educate, engage, and inspire you. However, its contribution to the grander rhetoric on psychedelics will not be what I have consciously offered in this book. It will be the insights and wisdom emerging in you as we integrate these experiences together.

Enjoy.

Stories are for telling.

2 FRIENDS, 5 GRAMS, AND A BOX FROM CUSCO, PERU

Freshly opened to the morning light, my eyes peered through a blurry haze to take first witness to the day. Awoken to my alarm, the events that lay forth ahead of me bore heavy implications in my thoughts. The plan was to connect with two friends and usher in the early afternoon by ingesting five dried grams of psilocybin mushrooms each. The looming anxiety of such a heavy dose was noticeably present, but the day was light and I felt ready for anything.

In the few months prior to this adventure, I had come to dedicate myself to writing a book. The goal was to create something to inspire others, and in turn take my creative passions and make them a career. This was in no way an easy task, and in order to maintain the dedication needed to see it through, I had constructed the perception that this book was somehow my purpose, my role in the world. In doing so, my commitment to this book had become a foundational element of my self-identity and the fuel for what would drive me to work on it every day. This was a pretty significant change for me, as except for videos games when I was in my early teens,* I hadn't been this dedicated to anything in my life. That lack of internal direction often left me confused and perplexed about the point of life in general. The shift from personal confusion into clear dedication was an epiphenomenon of my work with psilocybin mushrooms as a tool

---

* I had actually caught all 151 Pokémon.

for personal development. In fact, the book was inspired by my practice with the mushroom, and what this practice showed me about the nature of the human mind, emotional repression, and societal conditioning.

Somewhere along the course of this mushroom practice, in my mid-twenties, I began reading the work of a man named David Deida. He writes on spiritual sexuality, and his book on masculinity made a huge impact on my life. It had offered me the suggestion that people (men or women) who identify as having a masculine essence thrive when they dedicate themselves to a purpose, goal, or direction. It turned out that for me, this was true. Once I discovered what felt like 'my purpose,' I made it not only a goal, but a life path. I felt driven, nourished, and confident. This was the state of mind in which I was entering the psychedelic experience ahead of me, riding along the zephyr of having found and dedicated myself to something I believed was a valuable offering to the world.

Of course, the 'heroic dose' of five grams of magic mushrooms is intimidating regardless of what state of mind one is in. But I felt grounded and ready; in fact, a bit cocky. After thirteen months of taking relatively large doses of mushrooms by myself on a regular basis, I felt like this journey would be a breeze. That was a mistake, and a lesson in humility soon to be learned through personal crisis.

I woke early to ensure some time to prepare my mind and body for the day before I left to meet with my journey mates, Arlo and Trystan. I got up, meditated, showered, dressed, and headed to the kitchen to make some breakfast.

At that time in my life, I had yet to fully understand the role diet plays in one's experience of reality; how to pick and choose food according to what calibre of experience I was seeking to have was still a mystery to me. This day was a turning point in that dietary awareness, a result of having made what would later be realized as a terrible breakfast decision. The effects this breakfast had on my body, given the context of taking psychedelics that day, offered me a specific set of challenges that would eventually play a huge role in my relationship to breakfast for the rest of my life. I was still under the misinformation that the body needs 'fibre' from grains in the morning to get the digestive system working, so I started my digestive day with a toasted kamut grain bun with butter, jam, and hemp seeds, followed by a big bowl of oatmeal and a cup of black tea.* Turns out the necessity of grains for breakfast is false, and if the *high-healthy-fat* and paleo diet cultures are correct, the opposite maybe be true. But it wasn't the long-term consequences of this type of diet that made an impact on me, it was the short-term ones—it wasn't long before the bread and massive load of grains proved itself unwise.

I was already feeling the nervous anxiety of having such a big day ahead of me, and this type of anxiety often causes my digestive system to seize up. In this context, the giant ball of fibre I had just packed heavy into my intestines only served to exacerbate the issue. This digestive situation, my state of mind, and the limited time available to me before I had to leave resulted in me not have a morning bowel movement before I set forth to the psilocybin neverlands. This only got worse as time progressed as the imperative to release got stronger, and in a combination of emotions and poor dietary choices, I had constipated myself on the same day I was to eat an incredible dose of psychedelics. As you can probably imagine, this experience sucked. Its distinct discomfort, physically and psychologically, prevailed throughout the day. The mushrooms would later offer me an increased awareness of how intensely my state of well-being is affected

---

* In hindsight, it's pretty clear that the butter and tea were the only healthy breakfast choices I had made that day; breakfast fats and warm drinks for the win.

by having a gut backed up with unreleased waste due to being unnecessarily overinflated with the insoluble fibre of grains. The trail of realizations that came with this experience was potent to say the least, but I'll save the need for you to follow me through those challenges and leave *most* of the digestive specifics out of the story, I promise.

All packed up (pun intended), I left my home around 9:45am to catch the bus up towards Arlo's house, the physical vessel for my would-be ethereal explorations. The bus ride was short, and it was no more than ten minutes before I got off to walk the rest of the way, which again, was a rather short distance. Upon arrival, I found Arlo and Trystan sitting comfortably in the living room. It was a mild winter's day and the sun was shining through the large front windows, illuminating the room. If you have ever lived in a place where the winter lasts for a long time, you know what the lack of light can do to a person. So the fresh sense of life this winter sunshine offered to my weary seasonal heart was a blessing to have in the setting of such a powerful experience to come.

Arlo is a rather tall character with gorgeous brown dreadlocks that perfectly suit his physical grandeur as they hang from his head like the roots of a mighty oak tree. He is a very kind man, soft and relaxed, yet poised with a razor sharp wit. He and I met in some magically synchronistic community context that has slipped into the unplumbed and unreachable reservoirs of my memory bank. Yet, where we got to know each other was through a little tea house in a cute business district filled with the perfect combination of fringe culture people. Arlo and I 'hit it off' famously, indeed kindred spirits with a friendship to write home about.

Trystan is comparatively much shorter, with dark features and a penetrative gaze cushioned in gentle eyes. He is quite reserved on the surface but a man of potent wisdom once he is engaged. His body language is subtle, but the way he moves is as if he always has full-on psytrance music playing in his head. When first moving to Calgary, and before I actually met him, he always stood out in my mind as 'that really well-dressed guy who always smells fantastic.' Since the veil of peripheral social awareness had been lifted and I have explored a fuller understanding of who this great-smelling man actually is, I have come to trust him implicitly.

Arlo and Trystan: these were the two men with whom I was about to explore the edge realms of consciousness, an opportunity for which I was very grateful.

In the year leading up to this experience, all my psychedelic journeys had been exclusively solo. As mentioned earlier, I had been working with psilocybin as a personal development practice. My goal with this practice was to address and heal some self-deprecating identity constructs formed out of a significant period of destructive substance use. The deep personal work required to achieve my desired result seemed to be facilitated most effectively when I was by myself. I had found it a bit distracting to have the energies of another's emotional processes in my space, and so I journeyed exclusively alone. Yet, the drive to cultivate aloneness in my journeys shifted after about a year. In the private mushroom experience that was most recent to the one this story recounts, I was left with a message: *take a break from the solo journey and share this experience with others. Grow in relation to the growth of others on similar paths and create a point of reference for your lessons that extends beyond your own personal involvement.*

Somewhat serendipitously, it wasn't long after that message that Arlo and Trystan approached me, asking if I would be interested in joining them on a 'medicine journey.' Both of them offer reverence to the psychedelic experience as something to be had either alone or shared with mature and experienced others; people with this mindset are often hard to find. In a private discussion between the two of them, they had felt inspired to share such an experience with me and extended an invitation to journey together.

The context in which I learned of their inspiration was rather funny in hindsight, given its professionalism. They invited me over to their house for tea and talk, and halfway through looked at each other and nodded before introducing the idea and offering the invitation. I was honoured, and immediately felt a soft energetic nudge of intuition as if to say, "Do it." But before it was planned and decided, we discussed the intentions each of us sought to bring to the potential dynamic between us, our level of experience and mentality towards the use of psychedelics, as well as our personal philosophies towards their potentials. It was clear that there was a harmony between us, one that sang the sweet music of soon-to-be-shared psychonautic endeavours of the most promising type. We set a date, and finally, that date had come.

The sun had reached well past halfway in its transit towards dusk, yet the day still felt young as we were only just beginning. Establishing a sense of comfort between the three of us, we sat in conversation for a while, sharing tea and stories. We were opening ourselves into a mutual space of familiarity with each other and settling into that space before we took our dose. Investing this time to explore and set the dynamics between each other before dosing can be an important step to ensuring a healthy psychedelic experience.

Eventually, the space we were creating was complete and the time to take the medicine was upon us: five dried grams of psilocybin mushrooms.* We each sat in silence and prayer with our respective portions, subvocally communicating blessings of respect to the physical vessel housing the catalyst for the intense psychoemotional states of awareness we were about to unlock.

---

* As a point of consideration, these mushrooms entered our lives through a different friend who had brought them back from some magical wilderness woman they had met backpacking through the Canadian Rocky Mountains.

This expression of respect to the mushroom is an expression of respect to oneself, as that which is unlocked in an emergence of personal material, and is in my experience a valuable practice.

Each of us, at our own pace, chewed and swallowed our dose with nervous half-smiles and the obvious look of excited anxiety. I slowly chomped down on the dried pungent flesh of the psilocybe, swashing the resulting mush around my mouth before swallowing.

"To be honest, I've always kind of liked the taste," I said, being met with complementary opinions from both Trystan and Arlo.

I knew that mastication is an important step to digestion, and the more I broke down the cell walls of the mushrooms, the easier it would be for the psilocybin to be dephosphorylated and taken up into my bloodstream. Moreover, I assumed that the better I chewed, the lesser the gut rot. Magic mushrooms might take 1600+ dried grams in one sitting to physically overdose on, but it doesn't take much to cause me indigestion.

In experienced fashion, I brought along my yoga mat. Psilocybin mushrooms can be very intense, especially at the dose we had chosen. They release a rush of emotional energy normally repressed and stored in the physical body, mitigated by the higher-order identity constructs of the ego. The processing of this energy is directly related to the physical vessel it is flowing through; the movement of emotional energy is a movement of the body and vice versa. I have found that to better allow these intensified emotional energies to flow in a manner that facilitates the self-discovery, personal healing, and mystical epiphanies I prefer, a little body work goes a long way. Plus, doing yoga is a great way to redirect one's focus to a state of peace as the mushroom's onset briefly triggers the sympathetic nervous system into 'fight or flight.'

In the past, I would find myself overwhelmed by the novel

state of mind to which the mushrooms would bring me as their effects took hold and would expend a lot of mental bandwidth just trying to keep from losing my egoic sense of safety. Yet, as my personal practice took me in and through the deepest depths of my darkness and beyond into the divine self-visions of mystical oneness over and over again, this feeling of being overwhelmed was replaced by a feeling of coming home. It was this feeling of coming home that began to flow through me as I began to move through asanas on Arlo's living room floor. My body alive and engaged, I felt embodied, present in my meat suit and excited about feeling it move. There was a profound pleasure and nurturing in feeling the slightly uncomfortable sensations of stretch and release.

Experiencing the effects of yoga when in such a heightened state of mind has really allowed my practice to thrive. There is much one can learn about the broader potentials yoga can offer when it is practiced in those early stages of a psilocybin experience, when one is still able to manage calm, centered, and dexterous movements.

The inspiration to move and be movement itself was strong, but a stronger call brought me off the floor and back over to the couches to join Arlo and Trystan. While rolling up my mat, I noticed a simple wooden box off to the side of the longest couch, which sat across the opposite wall of the front windows. It was an untreated, lightly coloured wooden box, about three cubic feet in size, and stamped with red ink to show a smiling sun on the side and "Cusco, Peru" written directly beneath it. Maybe it was just a novelty bred of the increased firing of my locus coeruleus stimulated by the mushrooms, but this stood out as being an odd thing to have in a living room in Calgary, Alberta. The content and ambiance of this house hardly cheered normal, but still, I was so taken aback by the strangeness of this box that I had to ask about it.

"What's with the box?" I offered out towards Arlo.

"Oh yeah, that. It's a shipping crate. I have no idea where it came from but it's been here for months," he answered.

"Well… it came from Cusco, Peru," I stuttered as I giggled through the *captain obvious* tone I was speaking in. I stood there with this box, staring at it with the curiosity of a cat about to be killed and couldn't help but to look inside.

"What's in the box?" Trystan questioned as I peered under the lid.

"You don't wanna know," I responded in a cheeky tone.

I won't tell you what was in the box, but I'll tell you what I saw. I saw stories about banana crates from South America introducing weird spiders and cockroaches into Canadian grocery stores, and strange foreign viruses being unintentionally transported internationally. I saw an entire ecology of strange, foreign microbes invading the unprepared biological systems of a young Canadian on mushrooms. I saw danger.

Arlo's house of three young men wasn't the most vibrantly hygienic place I'd ever been, and the thought of these foreign microbes mingling and mutating in his home struck me as quite plausible. This thought quickly compounded upon itself as it was dramatically amplified in *meaningfulness* by my psychedelic state, swelling into an obtuse presence, and I was now officially uncomfortable about the box.

I looked over at Arlo. "That shit doesn't seem safe, it could have all sorts of strange bacteria and shit from South America."

"Bah, it's fine," Arlo nonchalantly responded. "I sit on it every day to tie my shoes."

"Well, Arlo, that shit freaks me out and I'm just not going to touch it again."

"Sure man, whatever feels right for you," was the not-so-assuring advice offered by Arlo as he and Trystan had a non-offensive laugh at my neurotic obsessive compulsiveness.

Arlo's living room had three sitting options: two armchairs and the couch that sat against the far wall from the front windows. One of the chairs and the couch matched in floral patterns printed across a forest-green background. With Trystan laying on the couch and Arlo on the odd chair out, I took my place in the comfortable green flower patch that sat closest to the mantelpiece at the far wall from the door, adjacent to the front window. Before I sat down in its cushion, I held the arms and gave it a strong shake.

"How strong is this chair?" I asked Arlo.

"I dunno, should be able to handle your body weight. Why?"

I briefly explained my current feelings of vibrancy and desire to be a part of the moment unfolding in action through physical expression, and that I wanted to be sure this chair could handle it. He assured me it could probably handle me as long as I didn't do anything too crazy, which I didn't plan on. I just wanted to be able to do a handstand on the chair and lift my body up into the air. Unfortunately, I had failed to recognize that I possessed a complete lack of ability to do such a handstand. When I tried, I ended up just twisting around to sit upside down in the chair, which I eventually got bored of and just sat up straight. Calmly sitting in the chair, I assumed that my flailing had come to an end. Little did I know at that time, I was about to put that chair through one hell of a test.

Both Trystan and Arlo have similar perspectives as I do about social conduct on shared psychedelic journeys. A space is created with others to allow for independent exploration and a secular respect for each other's individual process, engaging with each other when inspired to, but ultimately cultivating a personal experience. In these respects, time passed in a silence from spoken words as we listened to relaxed, progressive psy-trance music, and meditated.

I watched as Trystan sat up on the couch and brought his head in line of sight to my forward-facing gaze. The back of the couch came up to just under his shoulders, his head now comfortably placed between two paintings that hung about three quarters of a foot on either side of him against an off-white painted wall. The mushrooms had been in full effect for some time now and the familiar patterns of complex, iridescent geometry like a painting by Alex Grey began to paint a palace of psychedelic vision upon the once normal room around us. In a previous experience, I had come to recognize these patterns as the fundamental structure of the universe, as the framework upon which reality is constructed. In this moment, I directly experienced Neal Goldsmith's concept of material reality 'precipitating' from some underlying fabric of energy as a perceptual truth. I watched these patterns undulating around Trystan like an organic life form. They offered a sense of being totally present, yet only visible when I chose not to look directly at them. The patterns would fade away as soon as I began to stare upon them, emerging again as soon as my gaze softened. Their visual potency seemed to flow from Trystan and blossom into the room around us. Yet, the somehow sentient and integrated organic life form had no point of origin. It was present in between but permeating through everything in the room.

Looking at Trystan, I gave my absolute best but utterly failing attempt to describe what I was experiencing:

"I can see fractals of energy alive like fire. They are flowing all around us like an independent entity or life form, yet responding to you in some way. They change their shape and movements in relation to your thoughts and feelings. When you emote, they transform with a totally integrated responsiveness... It's so beautiful."

Trystan responded with a description of what he was seeing, though I can hardly do his words justice here and so I will not try. Please note, however, his descriptions had a very similar aesthetic and were eloquent and concise. So were Arlo's descriptions, as he offered up his visions as well.

Moments like these are profound and conceptually transformative, though in the flow of the psychedelic mushroom
experience, they are but stepping stones along a larger journey.
We sank back into a shared privacy for an indeterminable period
of time. I continued to enjoy the majestic play of visual energy
dancing around Trystan until nature called and I got up to use
the bathroom.

Due to the physical and psychological reasons previously
mentioned, I was still dealing with bowels full of discomfort. I
had hoped that this trip to the bathroom would free me of the
burden, but as I entered, I saw that it wasn't going to be that
easy. This was a house of several young men and at that point it
hadn't had a proper cleaning in a while. Walking up to sit on the
toilet, I couldn't help but perceive the trillions of dirt particles,
little hairs, and bacteria morphing and dancing with the clouds
of energetic geometry I was still visually processing. This new
set of fractals, however still beautiful in some way, made me
severely uncomfortable and my stomach began seizing up as if
to say "I'd rather not, please", but I was committed. This needed
to happen right away.

As I went to wipe the seat with toilet paper (a practice
merely symbolic and achieving nothing but minimal peace of
mind), the worst happened. The seat wasn't latched on to the rest
of the toilet and came right off. My face was now less than arm's
length to the rim of this seriously dirty toilet.

My olfactory and visual senses were greatly enhanced, my
reality was rendered of profoundly increased emotional and
psychological significance, and my entire bodymind was deep in
the psychedelic experience. Time froze as I bore full witness to
the speckled glory of that porcelain vessel for unspeakable life.

In a shudder and a cringe that shook me to my core, I was
freed of that infinite regress with a strong "nope, no way, not a
chance in hell" stated by my bowels. So I just took a piss (standing

up), felt some release in my midsection and resolved to wait till I got home to shit and never, ever enter that bathroom again. Problem solved, or so I thought.

While washing my hands, a bandage I was using to protect a wound lost its adhesiveness on one side and lay exposed to the air around it. I had accidentally sliced my thumb with a knife a few days before; the cut was in the crook between the knuckles, and though it wasn't deep, its location made for a tricky healing process. I had been treating it with some herbal wound care ointment and appropriate bandaging to help it gain back its strength. At this point in time, however, the wound would still open slightly every time I bent my thumb. It was not ready to be without protection and I was without an extra bandage.

I wouldn't consider myself a germaphobe, but I have a loose working knowledge of pathophysiology and a great imagination. In my mushroom-enhanced state, the gaps in my understanding of bacterial infection were hijacked by my imagination, and some not-so-subtle paranoia took firm hold. I did my best to calm myself down and rationalize the situation. Since I had already decided to never enter that bathroom again, that was no longer a concern. I figured that if I simply held the bandage on and stayed mindful of my wound for the rest of the afternoon, it would be fine. I convinced myself to be confident in this as a 'solid decision' and managed to calm down. Exiting the bathroom, however, I walked past the box on the floor to my right and that calm confidence quickly disappeared.

I went over to sit on my friend, the floral chair, and tried to relax into my experience, but I couldn't. I was being overtaken by the perception of that box having introduced foreign bacteria into this home; foreign bacteria that my body would not be able to recognize or handle, ultimately leading to an infection that no doctor could help me with because its origin was from South America. With no Western doctor able to help, I would be left to suffer a painful, life-threatening encounter with microscopic aliens in my bloodstream, probably dying or losing my arm to a flesh-eating infection of some sort. This was not good.

The established intention between the three of us was to cultivate a group setting that allowed for personal, private experiences. This is respected by staying introverted as to allow each other the opportunity to experience themselves without distraction. Yet at this point in my paranoia, I was in an overwhelming emotional state of panic and fear that warranted reaching out for help, so I asked Arlo if he had a bandage. He didn't.

There was looming danger in the room and its source was labelled "Cusco, Peru." It was clear to me that some strange, (probably flesh-eating) bacterial infection was in store for me if I didn't protect the integrity of my internal system from the contents of this dangerous polyhedron. This looming danger grew very quickly into an exquisitely irrational intensity.

I followed Arlo around like his shadow for several minutes as he gave a solid effort into finding me some level of wound protection. As we walked through his house on our fruitless hunt, its unhygienic environment—the bathroom and kitchen in particular—began to make me even more uncomfortable, uncomfortable enough to begin to rant at Arlo as to why I was so uncomfortable. Essentially, I was telling him I thought his house was disgusting. I would normally hold more tact, but the urgency of treating my body in that moment inspired some pretty tactless comments emerging from my anxiety.*

After the search for a bandage proved futile, we decided to improvise: paper towel and scotch tape. Certainly not the most hygienic option for protecting a wound, but anything that

---

* I have never asked Arlo how he felt about my expressions of overt judgementalism, but having learned about him as a person since that day, I imagine he took it in stride.

would guard me from the South American jungle bacteria that was swarming through the living room was going to do just fine for the time being. Unfortunately, there was a major problem with that plan. The only roll of paper towel we could find was sitting on top of the box. This just wouldn't do. I continued to push my mostly irrational urgency onto Arlo, explaining to him with the wide eyes of a panicked animal, "I just want to protect the integrity of my body from foreign invaders."

What felt like a long time of searching came to an end when I realized there was really nothing for me in his house. Releasing Arlo from my overzealous expectations of him helping to curb my eccentricity, I decided to accept responsibility for my own choices. I knew I had a cut on my thumb. I knew the bandage's adhesion was less than great that morning. I knew I was going on a psychedelic journey in someone else's environment, and I knew I didn't choose to bring any first aid with me. Whatever consequences were to come of those choices would be of my own doing. And so, I returned to the green floral chair from earlier to see Trystan still laying comfortably on the couch, seemingly undisturbed by the series of events unfolding around him, softly drifting in some psychic space likely bedazzled in geometric intrigue.

Holding out my hand and looking at the cut, I contemplated the best course of action for my personal protection. And then, for the first time since I realized my impending danger, I got out of my neurotic mind and asked my body what to do. In a flash of insight, I realized that my physical body was not some helpless machine just trying to run business as usual, but in fact, an integrative and living system that responded to my mental and emotional state. My flailing worry about the dangers of flesh-eating infections was hardly creating a constructive space for my body to do its instinctive duty of healing itself. If I wanted to stay safe in this context of lacking the necessary tools to protect myself on the external level, I needed to change my state of body/mind to best facilitate an internal protection.

Holding my injured left hand up near my heart. I laid back comfortably in my chair and zoned into myself. I entered a meditation, a type of self-hypnosis, wherein I connected with my immune system's central control and engaged in dialogue with myself. While cultivating the increasingly familiar emotional state of loving self-acceptance, I told my body the situation we were in and apologized for my lack of forethought. Simultaneously, I began forgiving myself for my mistakes and moving into a new space of constructive self-image. I let my immune system know that we were going to need to step things up a bit for the next few hours and send extra troops to the site of my thumb wound to keep the invaders at bay. Receiving a confident *Yes, sir* from my immune system, my confidence returned. I settled comfortably into the space around me and apologized to Arlo and Trystan for invading their personal space, for which they humbly forgave me.

The erratic series of events that had just taken place drifted naturally into what we understand as the past, and the ever-flowing moment entered a calm center once again, but not for long. The stereo behind me was sending out relaxed and rhythmic tones. Their vibrations seemed to slip down to the floor and slowly rise up into the atmosphere of the room, creating an ambiance of encouragement to journey within myself for the potential meaning of *what is*. Merely observing, non-attached to the stream of thoughts dancing to the beat, I drifted through my inner world with my eyes softly closed, though still periodically opening to take in the heightened beauty of the colours in the room. Thoughts and ideas came and went and the euphoric sensations of peace and intrigue washed over me, confidently singing *Wow, thank you.*

Meditation on psilocybin is a wonderfully unique experience. Normally I feel meditation helpful to clear out excess mental chatter. When on mushrooms, however, the act of meditation works as a platform to observe a flow of increased emotional awareness, rendering into intellectual thought automatically as the rational mind attempts to explain the emergence of abundant non-rational, emotional information. Manifesting as creative visual metaphors, these thoughts are often referred to as 'visions.' To navigate these visions during meditation with mushrooms, I often consider emotions as flowing like waves in the ocean and meditation like keeping balance on a surfboard.

Sometimes these waves come up and go down with little disturbance. Other times, the emotional ocean excites like a white squall and I'm just doing my best to surrender to the power of the water, with often futile attempts to remain steady on my board. This day's journey had become like a sunny day on a semi-tropical bay, and I was leisurely enjoying a float on warm inviting waters with friends nearby. Sitting comfortably in my chair, I rode these soft waves of insight until a great wave approached, triggered by a memory of a dream I had the night before. This wave was a big one, and before I knew it, I was up on my board and riding like Patrick Swayze in the final scene of that terrible film with Keanu Reeves where they robbed banks wearing masks of American presidents and celebrated by surfing.*

Like most dreams I happen to remember at some point throughout the day, it was fragmented and strange. I was in the busy night-time parking lot of a Walmart, standing around a blue car with a few friends. One friend, Kevin, came up to the group and he and I went inside. While inside the Walmart, we walked through the toys section and over towards the bikes. I can't remember exactly what we were talking about, but at some point, he turned into the Canadian Prime Minister, Stephen Harper, and I open-hand smacked him across the face. At first I

---

* *Point Break* (1991)

19

felt intimidated, thinking *Oh, shit, I just smacked the Prime Minister in the face. I'm gonna be in so much trouble.* But turning back into Kevin, he looked at me and told me it was okay, that he deserved it, which, if you happen to follow Canadian politics, you'll know, he did.

There wasn't much else to the dream, but I didn't really need much more than that for my psilocybin-enhanced perceptions to uproar with a stream of correlated significance. It went like this:

Kevin is a close friend of mine. The characteristics I often associate to him are conscious spiritual living and a deep understanding of internet technology. In fact, Kevin is my go-to guy for any technical or philosophical questions I have about the internet. Of my friend group, he has the most advanced, yet simply explained and openly shared understanding of the internet and the technology related to it. Stephen Harper is responsible for many atrocious legislative changes to what any intelligent and informed person would consider as vital Canadian infrastructure. I don't fully remember the details, but at that point in this dream, Harper and his cronies were in the midst of attacking the internet, vitally jeopardizing its integrity. In an incredibly fast-paced and complex series of connections, this led me to understand that the dream 'vision' rendering in my psychedelic experience was telling me that the internet was alive and under threat. Furthermore, the internet was communicating with me through my dreams because it and I and anyone else who is directly involved in participating in the greater internet community are subconsciously connected to it.

This sparked an explosion of energy through me as I fully embodied this exciting epiphany. I could feel a sentient, yet interconnected consciousness inside of me realizing itself as alive. I was experiencing a new form of intelligence coming into self-realization and saying hello to the world for the first time through me. This experience rose up in me and manifested at critical mass as a fury of animated elation as I laughed and announced to Trystan and Arlo, "THE INTERNET IS ALIVE!"

I was hardly able to make sense of much else around me as I reeled around in an excitement quickly emerging to the surface of consensual reality through deep, full belly laughs. Of course, my compadres had no idea what the hell I was talking about, so I tried to explain it to them. I outlined the internet as a living system that we have helped create through feeding it with our ideas and personalities to the point that now our injected human spirit has sparked life into it like lightning through the bolts in Frankenstein's neck (you can imagine the look of total bewilderment on their faces).

I was being thrown around in wild expressions of excitement bubbling through me like a volcanic eruption, punctuated with extremely brief moments of clarity and calmness. I attempted to apologize for invading Arlo's and Trystan's personal experiences once again, but I could hardly speak through the belly laughs. Trystan, still sitting in seemingly undisturbed calmness on the couch, assured me that it was fine while remaining mostly uninvolved in what I was going through. Arlo, on the other hand, chose (for better or worse) to engage me and participate in a mostly intelligible discussion about the nature of this revelation, while I did my best to explain it through the emotional furor.

It was in the midst of what might have been the most eccentric moment in my life when Arlo's friend Findlay showed up. The three of us were clearly out of our minds and the energy of the room must have been thick. Findlay came in, said "Hi," announced that his short stay was only to grab some audio gear from downstairs, and quickly left the room. Our (my) psychedelic

21

mania continued and Findlay happened to come back upstairs in the midst of another one of my giggle fits. Struggling to keep calm, I introduced myself from across the room and was met with an approving salutation before he quickly got himself away from our insanity.

Despite the induction of a sober mind into the mix, the energy of epiphany was still flowing inside of me and it was starting to be too much. In one of my brief moments of clarity, there was a second of gratitude for having checked the sturdiness of my chair earlier on, because I was really putting it through the works. I was bouncing up and down in it and shaking as if the world was laughing through me. I became the complete embodiment of the very same cosmic giggle that likely brought the universe into existence. I was reliving the big bang inside my belly and it felt amazing, but I couldn't handle it on my own anymore. Like a child having a fit, I slid off the chair and onto the floor. Arlo just happened to be nearby and on the floor as well. I reached out and grabbed his arm, channelling the overflow of this energy into him. As I laughed from the depths of creation, I saw his face light up as if I had plugged him into the charging dock of Zeus' lightning bolt machine. Both Arlo and Trystan began to laugh as I shook Arlo ferociously and shouted in his face "HOW DOES IT FEEL TO BE A PART OF LIFE REALIZING ITSELF AS ALIVE?!?!"

In too much of a frenzy to keep any kind of stillness, my craze was causing havoc all around us as I pushed Arlo over, almost tackling him, repositioning the coffee table by about forty-five degrees and knocking over his full pint of spring water onto the floor. Trystan, still on the couch, was now almost rolling in laughter at our complete loss of sensibility.

Oh fuck, I thought, as Arlo looked and me with a smile and said, "Oh great, now there's a lake on my floor."

Still in the midst of a mass of eccentric commotion, I made a quick scour for something to clean up this spill. The first thing in sight was the paper towel roll sitting on top of the diseased box, but there was no way in hell I was going to touch that, so I grabbed a nearby scarf (which I coincidentally found and pulled out of my floral chair before we ate our mushrooms) and began to sop up the mess. In playfulness, Arlo and I continued to yell feverishly at each other about the lake on his floor and why there was no way in hell I was going to touch that box to get the paper towel. In a crescendo of novelty, Arlo threw the soaking wet scarf flippantly up into the air and its wet weight crashed down upon the corner of the box's lid, flipping the lid diagonally to its corners and sending both the wet rag and the paper towel into its infested depths before the lid landed perfectly back on the box while all three of us jumped back from it in terror, screaming like six-year-old schoolgirls stumbling upon a massive spider at a sleepover.

Sinking back from hysteria in the wake of comical release, it came into awareness that Arlo's roommate was supposedly sleeping in the other room… oops. We yelled out an apology while we all sat looking at the box, digesting the intensity of what just happened. Staring at the box with watery eyes and sore cheeks, a new revelation came to me.

In the same manner that I was experiencing a connection with the now-living sentience of the internet, I began to experience a connection to the always-living sentience of the planet. I was engaging in dialogue with Mother Earth through the subtle thoughts emerging into my awareness. She was sending me a message:

> *As one who is now awake and aware of nature's intelligence, I have a responsibility to utilize this awareness for the betterment of all human, plant, animal, and fungal kind alike.*

In this message, I was also being given a mission: to destroy that box.

Immediately grounded by the gravity of my new mission, I looked stoically and seriously at Arlo and said, "Arlo, this box is introducing foreign bacteria that are unnatural to the ecology of Alberta and is a threat to the integrity of our environment. We have to burn this box."

Without hesitation, he looked equally as stoically and seriously at me, right in my eyes and said, "No."

"Dude, this is your responsibility as an intelligent member of this planet. It is your responsibility to your Mother Earth to set fire to this box and burn it to ash!"

"No," he stated again with an equal level of seriousness, but now with the look on his face as though he were bearing witness to absolute madness in front of him. "It's not even my box, it's my housemate's. I can't set fire to someone else's property."

I understood his reservations and encouraged him to call his housemate and ask him if it was okay, which was also met with a no.

Trystan, the calm Buddha in the midst of this psychedelic storm, offered up a vital question that neither Arlo nor I had thought of: "Where would you burn it?"

This question made sense, as it was a pretty big wooden box. Clearly, we couldn't burn it inside the house, and Arlo's backyard was a wild zone of naturally overgrown shrubs; hardly a place for a fire. Most importantly, we were all still extremely high on five dried grams of psilocybin mushrooms and should not have been, by any means, under any circumstances, starting fires.

I was still being called from within by the strong voice of Earth herself to accept this responsibility, but the reality of the situation made it clear that setting fire to that box was not the best choice at that time. I looked firmly at Arlo and asked him if he could promise me that within a week that box would be burned and we would live up to our responsibility as conscious beings on this planet (I actually said it to him with that level of hubris). He met my request with the promise to look into it and I promised to help him.

The intense dynamic of the room ebbed into a sense of resolution. We repositioned the coffee table and chairs back to where they belonged and moved on. It was almost as though nothing had really happened at all. Each of us was back in our original place, calmly sitting in silence. Yet, it wasn't long before we were clearly at that point in our journey where venturing off into the great outdoors was not only safe, but also necessary. The three of us had spoken earlier about singing ourselves off into the streets and towards a nearby park, and now, the time had come. Mind you, we were still high and it was winter outside, so a ridiculous amount of time passed before we actually had ourselves together enough to be outside. But when that moment came, it was embraced with vigour.

The three of us started in Arlo's backyard. His house was a cute little bungalow painted pink and was previously lived in by a couple for close to fifty years. It was pretty clear that they made it their love nest for the time that they were there. It even had a little bird house up on a pole in the front yard that was a miniature replica of the house. With that being said, it was now falling apart and its current tenants were likely to be the last before it would be torn down to build something new.

The backyard was a jungle of leftover gardening intentions, overgrown shrubbery, and the subtle vibe of multiple parties over the few years the boys had lived there. The main attraction in the yard was a huge tree close to the house. Its trunk divided into three large sections at about five feet up from the soil, each section being more than my hugging arms could hold. The tree reached up about thirty feet into the air, branching out in the vascular expression of the plant's lungs. It played a major role in my first impression of Arlo's house. The first night I had come over to check it out was during a pretty wild party. I ran into Trystan upon arriving and he led me out into the backyard to find Arlo and his lady lying elegantly in a hammock dipping into the nook between the massive arms of this tree, a beautiful scene and a memory that will likely stay with me as long as my memory itself does. Of course, it was now a much different scene; it was just the three of us, snow layered the earth, and the hammock was gone. The tree was a favourite of Trystan and Arlo's, who were both stoked to christen our outdoor excursion with hugs and hangs in this majestic plant being.

After saying my hellos to this tree with an honest hug, I stood back slightly with my left hand still gently touching the crackled bark of my new friend. Looking content, noble, and at home, Trystan stood up in the spiralled crevice of the tree's thick reach, which he had climbed into while I was hugging it. He had been in quite a quiet and private space all day, even while subject to my boisterous, boyish, booming bursts of laughter and demands to set fire to that box from Peru. His inward journey proved seemingly constructive to his psychoemotional disposition. When he engaged me, he spoke in a calm, lucid, and conscious tone.

Between the three of us, the context of our friendship seemed to be founded upon intelligent conversation, honesty, and mutual engagement in a way that helped to engender mutual growth. Given that context, a question like, "Where do you see yourself going in life right now?" wasn't an odd one. But when Trystan offered this inquiry, I was taken aback with no answer.

***

In order to understand why this question was about to take me through such a huge emotional loop, let me explain where I was inside of myself at that time in my life, the heuristic I used to interpret and understand my personal development and conflict with society. Pardon the overt academic and biographical tone to come.

At the point in my life when Trystan asked this grand question, I was relatively fresh into a new perspective on my life in general. Like most people raised by the public school system and cable television, I was brought up to internalize the Western stereotype of what it means to live a 'good life' and the clearly defined hoops one must jump through in order to achieve it. Essentially, it looks like this:

- Be as (institutionally) schooled as possible so as to become a skilled wage worker at a position in some previously established socio-business structure;
- Settle for garbage positions and wages until you have worked long enough to be content in the wage position you will eventually earn;
- With the money earned through this position, buy nice things to fill your life with artefacts of your hard work;
- Use those artefacts as evidence of your hard work to gain social acceptance and influence;
- It doesn't necessarily matter if you feel inspired, happy, or engaged by the actual work you do; all that matters is that you are satisfied with the financial, materialistic, and social results (and that you are always *better* than your neighbour);
- Wherein 'success' is determined by the quantity of said results and these 'successful' results are only available if you follow the previously established structures towards previously established or developing positions within the previously established social recognition of value;
- If you don't live this life, you will likely die sick, poor, and alone.

There may be some value in the founding principles in this social perception, but ultimately it is a psychosocial control system that tailors people into being good workers and consumers within the established socioeconomic system. This control system is facilitated through a psychological conditioning embedded, maintained, and perpetuated by the state-education system, television culture, socially accepted (and encouraged) drug use and addiction—alcohol, cigarettes, sugar, caffeine, television, and pharmaceuticals, especially antidepressants—and other people unconsciously acting as agents of control for the system through the induction of guilt and shame into others for behaving outside of the social rulebook. Mass cultural influence bred of the evolution of the military-industrial complex trains potentially creative vibrant human beings into *Business Professional Robots*.

Not everyone falls into this conditioning; many people see through it. Unfortunately, due to the forcefulness of this conditioning system, the people who see through it often respond with an equally as forceful polar reaction. They hate and denounce the system, and in turn throw away many of the functional and important principles that are woven into the control structures currently employed, such as working hard to achieve a goal, personal dedication, social connections, increasing quality of life, etc. Because of this polar reaction, instead of utilizing the aforementioned valuable principles to create social change for the better, many simply become self-serving *Flailing Hippies*, romanticizing freedom while living off the tit of those still working within the system. This is good for the system because the freethinkers and visionaries who could be creating important changes through building new conditions that no longer destroy inspiration and creativity, thereby evolving the structure we have, simply create perpetuating self-illusions of disconnection from the system while feeding and surviving off the leftovers of people still in the system.

28

Business Professional Robots and *Flailing Hippies* —these two extremes perpetuate each other. The *Business Professional Robots* push the freethinkers to become *Flailing Hippies* with their overt boundaries and forcefulness. The *hippies* push the *robots* to tighten their grip and strengthen their beliefs due to the sense of being attacked by the extreme polarity (and likely affluent judgment) created by the *hippie* lifestyle and its representatives. Then there are *hippies* who come and live off the people in the middle of the spectrum, people who are still connected to the system but trying their best to embody lasting creative change. These people are already challenged enough in this journey due to so much of their time spent just trying to keep their financial heads above water. These potential change creators only get pushed deeper into the system to make up for the hard-earned abundance energetically fed into self-serving *hippies*.

I know this is not everybody and that this dichotomy is generalized. These are extreme archetypes, caricatures, but in drawing these extremes we can get a better picture of where and how their subtle expressions manifest. We are also able to better see the feedback relationship between these two archetypal roles in current society. *Robots* create *hippies*; *hippies* create *robots*; both believe they know better; both are living a fallacy; neither create lasting positive change.

Personally, since adolescence I have always fallen towards the *hippie*. I saw through most of the bullshit in my social indoctrination and embodied the rebellion against it, like a good pawn should. Thankfully, I eventually began to see through my own shit and discover that there is a way to live a creative, passionate life that doesn't force me into a drab social compliance with what I have been offered or into 'running away' from my responsibility as a human to work towards creating a better world through accessible, local, social change. I realized that I could take the principles of commitment, hard work, and earning one's social value, while still embodying my creative passions to inspire others (and thus culture) into promising, lasting change. What you're reading here is an expression of it, as are the videos, articles, presentations, and social events I help create. It has been an extremely challenging process to discover, embody, and express what I feel are my creative gifts to the world and continues to be so. It has involved facing a lot of self-doubt, self-deprecation, the negative projection of potential 'failure' from others, as well as the cultivation of my skills, my gifts, and faith in myself. Yet, it has been a blessing to weather the storms that have come with it.

What I have learned from the challenges of this developmental process is that the internal narrative, the *language* operating inside my mind—inspired by my diet and habitat—is what will unconsciously direct my choices in action, thought, and feeling. These choices are what create the context for me to repeat or create new choices. My ability to create the life I wish to live and build the social niche needed to support that life while still participating in an energetic feedback loop of mutual abundance with the community that supports me is determined by the *language* programming embedded in my psyche. Part of the process of getting beyond the *robot/hippie* duality means deconstructing and reconstructing the established *languages* and conditions already present. This is one of the processes for which psychedelics, especially psilocybin, provides the opportunity. It is hardly an easy process and sometimes it means being completely knocked out of balance to find my feet again. This painful opportunity is exactly what Trystan offered me.

***

Where do you see yourself going in life right now?

Standing in front of Trystan perched in the tree, confronted by this deep question he offered, I became intellectually frozen. I reached within for all the *languages* I had been programming to navigate myself in moments like these, but they were all gone. I tried to answer with descriptions of publishing the book I was writing, travelling around to teach lectures on the philosophical framework I had constructed for the psychology of psychospiritual psilocybin use, travelling the world as a published author inspiring others, and so on, but nothing was there. Or clearer yet, it was all there, but none of it felt honest or real. Taken aback, struck with confusion and a loss of self-confidence, I was honest with Trystan and told him, "I don't know," as my heart sunk and a borderline panic filled my eyes. I was confused; normally it was all right there, ready and willing to be sung out into existence, but in that moment it was all meaningless.

Hoping to realign myself through his inspiration, I redirected the question to Trystan. I observed his stoic posture and listened as this deep, beautiful man spoke clearly about his intentions, yet I was anything but inspired. Not because he wasn't inspiring, but because I held my confusion in relation to his clarity and felt myself coming up short of the bar I had set for myself. Expressing a genuine support for his direction, I gently removed myself from the conversation as he and Arlo began to engage each other.

I wandered off solo to walk through the dilapidated and snowy backyard garden. It had likely once flourished with organic life, cultivated with love. But that was no longer the case and I could relate. Even with all the experience I had developed in my practice with psilocybin, I was still subject to its challenges. I began to sink into the emotional lull of questioning myself and my direction in life; my cockiness of the morning was laid to waste. The massive nature of the challenge that had presented itself had me feeling defeated. Essentially, *figure out who you are, what is it you are trying to create in your life, and how you are going to go about doing that.*

If you haven't experienced psilocybin mushrooms it might be difficult for you to understand how a challenge like this is experientially presented. For me, it's not a clear question outright, but an emotional state that swells inside of me and into my conscious mind as my intellect desperately struggles to make sense of its implications. I have learned that this process can be of great benefit in life if one can learn how to use it. In my experience, the only way to do this is to absolutely *surrender* to the depth of the emotions emerging. Whether comfortable or not, embrace it; take note of the ideas that arise, ask questions, and trust in the honesty of the emotional experience as it unfolds. I know these things in my sober mind and have applied them multiple times within my psychedelic experiences. Yet, even with all this understanding, I can still find myself confused and unsure of what to do with myself once I'm in the direct moment of facing turbulent and dark emotional states with mushrooms. It can be tough to think clearly when so overwhelmed.

The three of us left towards a nearby park with the intention of following its path all the way through to the cemetery at the other end. Something about the metaphor for life that this specific direction offered seemed relevant to the context of our experience that day.

Conversation was flowing well between my two compadres, but I kept mostly silent. I was in a deeply uncomfortable emotional state that was impossible to avoid, despite my efforts. I did my best to keep up with the topics moving between Arlo and Trystan instead of surrendering myself to the challenge that had arisen. Regardless of this effort to keep up, I only sank deeper and deeper into a sullen melancholy regarding my life. Instead of allowing these emotions to flow naturally and let an understanding of them come through their natural process of catharsis, my mind was running with attempts to curb this inner turmoil.

I walked a few paces behind the guys as we meandered our

way through the long and winding walkway that weaved the well-designed, but clearly tailored beauty of Confederation Park. Every now and then I would try to join in on the conversation, only to hit a strong block. Unable to speak, I'd stutter, pause, apologize, and step back. "I... uh.... I.... I'm sorry, I can't." Thankfully, I was with two companions who lovingly accepted and respected my inabilities at that moment. They gave me the space to process and not feel alienated or judged. These are the kind of friends who I can trust during a psychedelic encounter with personal darkness.

In my mind, I was being shown all the things I wanted with my life, the great challenges they would require, and the huge blank space that stood between myself and the life I wanted to create. Lost and confused about my direction and purpose, I examined how I was going to do the things that I loved, which brought me very little money, and still be prepared to have a child at some point in the future. Artistic projects; unemployment; lack of a romantic partner; my family on the other side of the country; my involvement and role within my community; the prevailing socioeconomic paradigm I was born into; the looming economic collapse; the financial elite's manipulation of social structure; the potential of consciousness evolution, total destruction, or absolutely nothing in this upcoming year of 2012; personal health challenges; and the vital importance of food and water in general—all these things compounded onto me as problems I felt I needed to solve right there and then. The finer details and grander forces affecting how these challenges related to my life context and why their implications totally overwhelmed me aren't really necessary for this story, but trust me when I tell you that it was a very difficult walk through the park that lasted an experiential eternity.

Then, finally, it clicked in that I didn't need to figure out my entire life right then. I was high on psychedelics and emotionally overwhelmed. All I needed to do was appreciate the perspective I was being offered and be compassionate with myself in the midst of my existential crisis. That was a realization I have kept with me and since then has supported me through numerous challenges, both in psychedelic experiences and everyday life.

The weight on my soul began to lighten enough to connect with Arlo and Trystan. Of course, I wasn't ready to explain what was going through my head right away; I didn't actually know what was happening or what to do about it other than *surrender*. So, my first real contribution to the conversation between us was the only thing I felt confident in: I was hungry. The idea of food was now introduced into the group discourse and our pace towards the cemetery quickly slowed. We were pretty far from any kind of grocery store and after about forty minutes of walking, we were only halfway to the cemetery. We decided to prioritize food and turn back the way we came, head to Safeway for supplies, and return to Arlo's to cook dinner.

The uncomfortable space I had been swimming in over the last little while was finally able to be communicated, and it was met with understanding and embrace. I shared with Arlo and Trystan that I was in a pretty heavy emotional space and at some point might need to go off on my own to process it. I also apologized if my heaviness was weighing them down as well, to which they responded with loving support and acceptance.

As I managed to *language* my challenges and express my low self-esteem and self-confidence during the walk to Safeway, I was gifted with insight and support. It was Arlo primarily who addressed my concerns and did so in a way that eased my pain and helped me feel comforted. He provided a deep wisdom in his words that I can't and won't attempt to repeat. Most importantly, however, both he and Trystan offered me a sense that it was okay to be exactly who I was right then, challenged and all, because I was still loved and accepted. They helped me stand back into myself and offered me the tools to go from there; this surely was the most important thing I could have been offered in that moment.

Again, these are the kind of friends who you can trust during a psychedelic encounter with personal darkness. The kind of friends you can rely on as tribe on the journey towards psychospiritual maturity.

The story continues to flow from here towards a neurochemical homeostasis as we finally made it to Safeway after a very long walk. Initially, I went inside with them, only to realize that I was grossly unprepared for a mall-stationed grocery store at 5:30pm on a Friday evening. I encouraged them to leverage my insecure uncertainty and get whatever was needed for dinner while I waited outside, summated as: "I can't handle this right now."

Finding a small corner to sit in, I placed my hands on my heart and began to meditate. This was what I had needed the whole time, an opportunity to just sit and be present with myself. I breathed with intention, bringing forgiveness and compassion on my inhalations, releasing tension and stress in my exhalations. I didn't avoid my hard feelings anymore, but sat with them while cultivating a sense of worthiness and self-love. It must have been at least fifteen minutes before the guys emerged from hunter-gathering our dinner out from the chaos that is an affluent Canadian food supply chain store during rush hour. And by that time, I was feeling much better.

We shared dinner (a vegetarian curry) and conversation as I increasingly came back into myself and further understood why and what I had gone through. Still shaken, I shared my feelings and experiences openly with Trystan, Arlo, and Arlo's housemate Drew (who I suppose was with us most of the day, since he was the one sleeping in the other room). Like in most challenging psychedelic experiences that are given space to process naturally,

I came back into my centre and calmed down.

From experiencing life realizing itself as alive through my ego, battling foreign bacteria from a box that Mother Earth told me telepathically to incinerate, connecting subconsciously to the newly awakening intelligence of the internet, and navigating my way through a complete personal crisis, it was a long day and I was tired (and I still hadn't had a bowel movement). The effects of the psilocybin were no longer running through me, but the effects of the experience still held a deep presence as I gratefully hugged my fellow intrepid, psychonaut brethren goodbye and made my way home and into my bed. Shaken but strong, I slept well that night.

Psychedelics are powerful substances and not for the weak of heart. They can lead you into mystical bliss and drop you into the depths of your own shadow. But ultimately they are among the most powerful tools we have for personal growth when we use them responsibly and with mature intent. The few days following the intense wave of high and low encountered on this journey led me to some profound perspectives on why I encountered the challenges I did. Allowing myself a space to properly integrate my experience, I offered myself inspiration to a whole new series of creative ideas and projects, including this one.

In hindsight, the few weeks leading up to this journey and the moment wherein I was confronted by Trystan with a question to sink me for hours to come, were constructive. I had hit a point within myself where I knew where I was going and was working towards it diligently. I was working so hard and efficiently on my book project—*Decomposing The Shadow*—that I had lost sight of what was ahead of me. There was a firing of the coals in my action center and I was moving with an amazing pace, but as Trystan and the psilocybin showed me through catalyzing an emergence of uncomfortable emotional honesty, I hadn't bothered to really look at what was coming up on the horizon after such high-energy forward movement.

I was headed straight into a brick wall. I had no idea where I was going beyond my small view of completing the book, and this personal crisis was the emergency brake pulled, rearing this train to an abrupt stop, and the anguish that came with it was my ego trying to say *no, keep going*. It was certainly dark and challenging, though it gave me the perspective that this stop, when I eventually allowed it to happen, would open for a fuller grasp on my intentions and direction in life. Through the few days directly following this experience, as a part of my integration process, I took some time to write down my long-term goals and evaluate what was really meaningful in my life. This offered me some solid perspective and a level of self-confidence I had yet to realize I was capable of.

I finished the manuscript to my book and handed it off to an editor, started (and completed) a new essay discussing the vital role the internet is playing in our psychosocial and spiritual evolution.* In short, I began solidifying the next steps in my personal growth, life, and career.

In this moment and through these words, I hold infinite gratitude once more for close friends and the psilocybin mushroom as a personal teacher.

---

*This essay is titled *Technological Organism* and is available for free through my website at jameswjesso.com.

Integration

The experience of the internet waking into self-awareness may seem obscure, but looking at the symbolism and progression of it, the premise is pretty clear. By exploring the implications of what it would be like if the internet—a system of information reception, distribution, and organization—woke into consciousness, I was offered perspective on our place—humans—as being an expression of the same type of information system created by the planet and come into self awareness. In the same way that I felt responsibility to protect that life I had helped create as it was expressed in relation to the political threat posed on the internet, I felt a responsibility to protect the thing that created us; the natural evolution of the planet earth. This seems to be a prevailing theme among psilocybin use; that we are somehow stewards of this beautiful paradise we have manifested within, and that once we have this awareness, it is our responsibility to uphold this role to our greatest integrity, the cost of not doing so being a cost we pay with our lives and the lives of our children, grandchildren, and great grandchildren to come.

As an expression of upholding this responsibility, about a week after this experience, the three of us followed through on the mission we were offered by Mother Earth. This was comparatively insignificant to the problems we are facing as a whole planet, but contextually, we offered our word to what felt like the essence of the earth speaking directly to us, and the symbolism of respecting that in this small ritual had great value. It is the small things we do that add up to the mass of humanity's effect on planetary integrity.

Arlo confirmed with his housemate that we could burn that box from Cusco and arranged a place to do so. Some friends of his were having a gathering that included the intention for a campfire. He got their permission to invite Trystan and me, and bring the box to be burned.

The location where we planned to burn this box was about a fifteen minute walk from Arlo's house. Arlo, Trystan, and I took turns carrying the box to its final resting point, along the way, laughing and recounting our experiences and discussing the implications those experiences offered in our integration processes. Once we arrived, we brought it to the fire pit in the backyard, packed it full of kindling, and celebrated life with a ritual box burning.

Each new step increases in complexity and furthers the depths of darkness available for access.

DISCOVERING THE TRUE LIGHT
OF DARKNESS

Over the last few years, my relationship to the psilocybin mushroom has come to a foundation of gratitude, trust, and a healthy sense of intimidation. This relationship has brought me to directly face and address the culmination of some of the most guarded parts of myself. Dissolving the defensive postures in my psyche, it has helped me to explore patterns of deep-seated emotional hurt from which I had all but completely dissociated. It has also brought me in and through some of the most emotionally challenging experiences of my life. Through offering me confidence, courage, and release, it has been a profound and supportive medicine for me. It has helped me learn about who I am, why I am who I am, and who I can be if I choose it.

I have jumped with both feet into facing all that I unconsciously hide from, over and over again. I have allowed myself to be beaten by the mushroom's oft-unbearable honesty, each time going as deep into myself as I could, trusting that I would make it back to baseline before they broke me completely. Each time, I emerged with a new perspective on myself and my challenges, awakening from their immersive effects with a perceivably definite hold on the ambiguous concept of personal healing and an abundant gratitude for all that they offer. Yet, even with all these experiences under my belt, I am subject to their throes, and in the midst of their great challenges, I often forget how the story usually ends...

I learned what the mushroom had to offer me when I was

twenty-four years old and living in my parents' basement in the town I grew up in. After a period of uncontained, reckless drug use in Melbourne, I left to Thailand to 'find myself,' but only found further confusion. After eighteen months away, I was holding a scrambled sense of self and an archive of shameful secrets when I returned home to Ontario to live with my family. My mind was riddled with self-deprecating narratives about the nature of myself, narratives held up by a prevailing sense of fearful hopelessness about life in general.

The culturally familiar dynamic established between me and my parents during my coming of age was that of 'needing' to hide things to protect them (and myself) because they 'didn't understand.' Having returned from my travels, broken from so many reckless decisions, this dynamic was the palpable tension between my honesty and my relationship with them. I was so sure the truth would break my mother's heart and I would lose the respect of my father. I was afraid to ask them for help, afraid to come clean about what was happening and why. Of course, this prevailing perception of necessary secrets may have been seen as false if I had placed it in the light of five years living on my own across the world, but I couldn't risk it. I was too fragile; I needed to hide the truth from them. So I did, and sought help elsewhere.

Mostly inspired by listening to Terence McKenna and spiralling down the YouTube abyss of videos on psychedelic neo-shamanism, I found myself inspired to seek help from psilocybin mushrooms. Using one of my favourite recreational drugs to heal from the results of using too many drugs? It seems like a ridiculous rationale, but it felt right and I went for it. With desperate wings flown on the hot air of the Irish maverick McKenna's spoken word on jungle healing and fungal intelligence, I reached to the mushroom as though it were my spiritual teacher, a healer, a medicine. And so began my journey, once a month, always during the full moon, always by myself. I would eat four dried grams of the strongest psilocybin mushrooms I could find. The medicine in my system, I would go to the park to meditate, integrate, and explore my emotional wounds.

After thirteen months of this practice, I was different. I was generally happy, living in Alberta, had a great job, was building a wonderful community around me, and felt aligned with my creative passions. Finally, I was inspired again. It turned out, woven into the fantastic fabrics of intergalactic and seriously unrealistic propositions, that McKenna guy really had something valuable to offer. Given the observable changes in myself, I figured I must have addressed most of my primary mental health issues, and so I softened my commitment to the monthly ritual I had built for myself. It was clear that the next step for me was to explore my new relationship with mushrooms by engaging with them in different contexts than the full moon alchemy of my thirteen-month investment.

Since then, I have come to use the emotional ambiance of my life and the events that flow through it as the marking point for when it is time to explore psychedelics. I have let go many of the assumptions about 'spirituality,' 'healing,' 'ceremony,' and other belief systems I once held on to with a desperate investment, and have embraced a more pragmatic approach to my usage: *Where am I in my life right now? What am I seeking to achieve with my psychedelic use? What set, setting, and dose will best help me achieve this?* Typically, my journeys these days are structured with mature intent and a focus on personal healing and self-exploration, though not always. To think that there is only one way to obtain benefit from this medicine is shortsighted; a shortsightedness I have come to realize as having previously been a limitation in my practice with it.

As for the journey I am about to share with you, at that time I was still holding many of these aforementioned assumptions about spirituality. It was approaching December 21, 2012, and the community I interacted with was alive and electric with new age idealism around what '2012' represented, and to be honest, I was too. Regardless of whether or not the specific predictions people were making came true, I noticed beautiful changes in many people and in myself. The process of navigating the potential implications of the supposed "great shift of 2012" actually helped me fully explore what it meant to commit myself to my dreams. There was something about 'it could all be over soon' that really got me to focus on my goals, while simultaneously broadening my world to consider the question of what it meant to be human and alive. Even still, sometimes I ask myself, "If I were to die in only a few days, what would I need to be doing right now to feel like my last few days were worth it?" This story is an expression of me living the answer to that question, as writing and sharing stories is what I feel I have to offer the world.

For this story, the setting was early winter of 2012. There was snow and it was cold. What I experienced on this journey felt like a message that needed to be shared with everyone. There was a party planned at my house the following weekend and I spent four days locked in my room writing, editing, and preparing it as a gift to the people coming. I printed twenty-five copies of it, poorly edited and honest to its core. All those copies are gone now and I don't even have one. This version of the story has been polished, edited, and revamped in the light of hindsight and the development of my skills as a writer. But the honesty remains strong, as without it, this story means nothing...

Trystan and Arlo were now my housemates. Along with a beautiful woman named Sia, the four of us all lived in a welcoming home with vaulted ceilings, an open concept living room with hardwood floors, and a birch tree out front. The dynamics in our home were that of trust and confident vulnerability with each other; in many ways, we were and still are a family. Trystan and I were in our kitchen one night, talking and sharing openly, standing around a boiling pot of Chinese medicinal herbs. As the conversation unfolded between us, it came out that we had both recently been facing some noticeably deleterious anxiety in our lives, bred of nebulous challenges. Trystan and I are in similar schools of thought regarding mushroom use during bouts of depression, as we have both experienced depression as a very effective time to utilize their healing potential. As such, it wasn't out of the ordinary for this realization of mutual challenge to lead to the decision to share in a journey with psilocybin. Thus, we established a time and committed to four grams each.

For me, the imperative behind this decision came from a nagging emotional malaise pervading throughout most of my life. Something felt fundamentally wrong inside me and I couldn't put my finger on it. I tried to find solace in my social life, but I was genuinely uninterested in going out or talking to people at all. Even when I did go out, I felt alienated and uncomfortable, like I just wanted to go home. I was generally depressed without any clear reason for it. It was as though nothing really offered me satisfaction or excitement. I was unhappy. It was, for me, the perfect time to open my emotional floodgates with psilocybin and get to the root of my issue.* And knowing that I wouldn't need to face it completely alone gave me a sense of support.

From my journal just before we began:

> *I am about to embark on a journey, the breadth of which I have yet to grasp, but the necessity of which feels grand. Over the last week or so I have been overwhelmed with an unfortunately familiar sense of brokenness, one that has caused*

---

* I speak often about having healed through the depression of my mid-twenties with mushrooms, but they aren't a miracle cure. I am still human and vulnerable to the relative suffering of human existence.

me much grief and challenge. A feeling of being drained and disconnected, self-alienated and awkward in public feels jarring and all-encompassing. We are approaching the date 12.21.2012 and though my skepticism levels are high, so much is happening in my own life as well as on the global stage that I am starting to wonder if something IS happening, something well beyond my ability to comprehend. I clearly don't know what this something is, but it feels important and I wonder if there is something I need to BE, to be open to what is happening. Maybe I'm already BEING that openness and these dark feelings of late are a part of the process? Maybe this whole line of inquiry is all self-perpetuated illusion and I'm worrying over a fantasy? Maybe this has nothing to do with 2012 and I am simply attaching my depression to a common cultural meme to make sense of it or to evade personal responsibility for it. I don't know but either way, in this journey, I am seeking perspective on my low-density energy, healing from whatever wounds this is sourced in, and some direction in moving forward.

Before we ate our mushrooms, Trystan and I took some time to solidify a bond of mutual trust between us. We openly shared with each other the mindset with which we were entering this experience, our reasoning behind it, our hopes and fears. Doing this really helps to cultivate a sense of being understood and supported, as the mushroom experience can sometimes turn to the dark side very quickly, and a bond of trust with a journey partner may make the difference in a healthy integration.

This preliminary conversation established a sense of comfort between us; we were as ready as we could be, and so we sat quietly while listening to soft music and ate our mushrooms. The effects were slow to come on and I was thinking to myself that maybe I hadn't eaten enough. This is a tricky line of questioning for the intrepid journeyer, as the decision to eat more may immediately, upon completion, be recognized as a mistake when the experience becomes 'too much.' Considering my unstable state of mind when entering this experience, I certainly didn't want to find myself in that situation. I decided to just welcome whatever intensity may come and did some yoga to open and prepare my body.

As the first layers of mushroom awareness began to animate my reality, I sat up straight on my yoga mat and postured myself into seated meditation. A feeling of familiarity for this mind state emerged; it had been developing in each of my progressive journeys and continues to prevail since then. Being able to precisely *language* it is difficult, but this feeling seems to offer me the perspective that the state of awareness occasioned by mushrooms is in some way inherent to human consciousness and ours to harness. But first, there is a requirement of accepting the responsibility of this level of consciousness through embodying our role as stewards for this planet, getting over our ridiculous self-importance and simply embracing reality, whatever that means.

Sitting comfortable in this familiarity, I breathed into the awakening awareness of energy flowing in my body. This is another common theme for me; mushrooms seem to open the capability of directly perceiving internal energetic currents, like Chinese meridian systems. These energetic sensations in my body dominated my awareness and developed in their clarity as the mushrooms took fuller effect. I didn't try to understand this experience; I knew it was part of the process of coming up on a psychedelic and that my thinking mind's role at the time was to simply allow it to happen while staying calm, which I did by directing my breath as a means to this calmness and to cycle the perceivable energy in my body. Mindfulness and active engagement of the energetic sensations mushrooms catalyze have been a great way to maintain a sense of centeredness during the often turbulent intensity of their onset. But while directly attending to these sensations, I had to be conscious of not letting the rational aspect of my mind take over. It would only attempt to constrain the experience into one label or another, into some concept or philosophy. That precise moment was beyond the logical or rational; it simply was exactly what it was, and trying to make sense of it would only offer an anxiety I wasn't interested in creating.

It had been about an hour since we ate our mushrooms and we had come into the first fullness of our experience. The lights were low in the living room and we were sitting comfortably in a fort we had created on the floor with multiple futon mattresses and piles of pillows. We were silent with each other; the space we had created was intended for personal work, not necessarily conversation. The melodic ambiance of the room was being orchestrated by some wonderfully downtempo electronic music Trystan had put on the stereo just before we initiated our explorations.* Our stereo system had five speakers and a subwoofer, and so the sounds filled our environment from all directions and rumbled through the floor. Its progression and harmonics acted as a guiding force for conducting my still-growing sensations of energy. I could directly feel the harmonic interference between the resonance of the mushrooms—a unique frequency produced by the bioelectric state of my body and mind—and the undulating sounds of the music. It was gorgeous, and even more so, in the dimly lit ambiance of our pillow fort, I could see these interference patterns too. I was watching their iridescent beauty paint the normally empty space around me with kaleidoscopic patterns of seemingly impossible angles, drifting with bliss inside of myself.

The album was short and its finish marked an ebb in my onset effects. I got up to put on some other music, something

---

* Senzar – Before The Morning Sun

that I have since learned is not my preference; it is far better to establish the entire set of music in advance, if any, so that there is no urge or distraction with trying to change or decide new music.

My first few steps were a bit wobbly, but the responsiveness of my balance maintained my ability to walk, even though it felt more like floating. The music situation was under control and being that I was already up, I headed to the kitchen for some tea. I had begun preparing some herbs in hot water earlier that day, knowing that by this time they would be ready to drink. The smell of my soon-to-be cup of herbal warmth tantalized my nostrils the moment I entered the kitchen. It sparked the realization of how excited I was to explore the sensually dynamic experience it was about to offer.

Cup in hand, I calmly made my way back to Trystan through the bedazzled haze of the living room. Being slightly anxious but mindful not to spill my tea or bump into anything, a beautiful sense of relief washed over my body as soon as I relaxed into my seat. Settled on a pillow throne, breathing myself back into centre, I began to engage the fresh sensations and alterations in my awareness being catalyzed by the harmonic resonance of this brew.

Crafting teas is an art form, and this was not just any tea; this was my favourite blend to drink while on psychedelics: reishi mushrooms, goji berries, and gynostemma leaves. Tea has far more potential than just flavour; plants have intelligence and many lessons to offer us once we learn how to listen. Normally, it's a challenge for me to understand them, but while exploring the awakened realms of psilocybin-enhanced consciousness, the information offered is clear, concise, and communicated through a non-verbal *knowing* rendered as an intelligible narrative in my head. Both the reishi and the goji are highly revered in Taoist and traditional Chinese medicine. The reishi, or *ganoderma lucidum*, is said to be 'the herb of spiritual potency,' slowly dissolving the barriers that prevent us from embodying our inner wisdom. It is

51

very, very bitter and tends to be an acquired taste. The Goji berry, or *lycium barbarum*, is said by many to be a 'teacher,' offering the student the ability to better understand and integrate the wisdom of plants. It has a wonderful flavour and is also said to help with the maintenance of heart health and hormonal balance. It also has antioxidants, such as beta-carotene and zeaxanthin, which specifically help with maintaining healthy eyes. Gynostemma is a wonderfully flavoured adaptogenic herb that allows for clear thinking and eased digestion, along with producing a double-directional modulating effect on the metabolism, encouraging our metabolic states into balance with the contextual needs of the body. It is a pleasant and soft tea that sits very well with the reishi/goji combination, balancing out the reishi's bitter flavour quite nicely.

I sat with the cup close to my face as the vapours rising off the hot drink filled my nostrils with warm, moist air. Breathing with a mindfulness of my relationship to this tea, I opened myself to perceive whatever changes may occur in my sensory experience. I focused on the information it had to offer, its flavour, its smell, and the warmth of the cup in my hand. Plants don't speak with words, they speak with phytochemicals and pheromones and to listen sometimes means to smell and to taste. The structural geometries in my visions were modifying form, and the emotional manifestations of the energy flowing through my system as I drank and connected with the herbs in this tea took a noticeably new direction. Things were changing. My internal state was shifting, ambiguously at first, but with a clarity steadily emerging. I had connected with the essence of these plants as I communed with them through a mindful engagement of their experiential qualities. Intuitively, I began to directly communicate with their intelligence. I formed an inquiry with my intellect and directed it to the elements of myself that I felt were associated to those plants in that moment. I directed a question to their energy manifesting inside of me and opened myself to receive an answer.

Other than physical and emotional well-being, is there some grander purpose or benefit for us to connect with medicinal herbs in our diet?

At first the answer came as a soft energetic shift, a gentle emotional hum. But as I relaxed and surrendered my rational doubt as to whether or not the plants could really talk to me, an element of my internal monologue began to translate shifting emotional information as a verbal language. A narrative spoken through a foreign tongue inside of my head began to emerge, and I somehow understood what it was saying. It told me that every element of life on this planet holds a vibrational resonance or tone, and that the reality we normally interact with is merely the level of *surface consciousness*. Within that experience of surface consciousness, our reality is constructed from the perception of only a small section of frequencies within a much grander spectrum of potential. Furthermore, the frequencies that are perceivable to the individual are determined by the vibrational frequencies of our biological system, the resonance we emit. Our vibrational resonance is the culmination of our thoughts, feelings, actions, and the biochemical and physical operation of our body energetically expressed like a seamless orchestra. This personal resonance acts like a tuning fork for the full spectrum of reality, and we can only perceive the frequencies of reality that are harmonious to our vibrational resonance. These perceivable frequencies are rendered by our sensory nervous system and given place and meaning by our ego; everything else is omitted from experience. Herbs like reishi and goji, among others, are important because they have a vibrational resonance that, once ingested, alter the resonance we emit. Over time this changes us—biochemically, physically, emotionally, psychologically, and spiritually—to emit a vibrational resonance that opens us up to perceiving a broader spectrum of reality.*

This process of altering our personal resonance extends beyond our independent selves and out into the world around us. When we begin to emit this new resonance, inspired by the herbs we are ingesting, we generate a frequency field around us that is communicated to others *morphogenetically*,† which subtly alters their reality spectrum as well. I was starting to see that the reason these herbs are becoming so popular in contemporary society is because they are a part of a grander process that is awakening us to a fuller understanding of the nature of existence and potentiating our inner wisdom. They are helping us to be aware of the changes that are happening to the energetic substrate of reality as we evolve to an entirely new expression of life in the universe, a technologically advanced yet spiritually awakened humanity. Apparently, this is the grander purpose behind ingesting them.

I'm not sure what pulled me out of my conversation with the tea, but something did and when I went back into meditation, the nature of my experience changed dramatically. It was at that moment that I understood how intensely powerful the experience was becoming. Even in the light of all the psychedelic sensations, visions, and the ontological revelations received from the plants in my tea, the mushrooms had still been perceivably gentle. But that was over. With an amplified emotional potency, I was becoming aware of the unconscious source of the depression and social resistance I had entered into this journey with the intention of facing. I saw that I was starved for real, deep human interaction.

---

* I wrote a detailed essay outlining this concept called *Soundscapes & Psychedelics*. It is available through www.soundscapesbook.com.

† Based on the work of biologist Rupert Sheldrake, *Morphogenetic Fields* are a non-material latticework of energy that allows for the unconscious transfer of energy and information between different organisms.

And yet, I was the source of the choices that were alienating me from the rest of the world. I had no idea how to fix it and no idea why I was doing this to myself. I began to sink into a very dark and uncomfortable experience of regret and defeat. The mushrooms brought my depression to its fullest and it filled me completely.

The mushrooms sent me tumbling, lost, in a downward spiral of inadequacy, of not being good enough, of being a failed human. I knew on some level that the ego-narrative perpetuating the defeatist interpretations of these emotions was likely bullshit, but the practical application of that knowledge was completely unavailable.

Being able to just accept myself for who I was on my own accord seemed like a distant impossibility. I needed some help, an example of what it meant to just be oneself and worthy of love without the need to meet some expectation. It was clear to me then that there was no human in the world who could show me this, because we are all in the same boat of trying to prove something to someone at varying degrees of investment. It was so utterly clear to me that the only thing that would offer me the support I needed was a tree: I needed to hug a big, beautiful tree. I know this might sound weird to some of you, but in my heavy heart it was obvious that the strong welcoming honesty of a tree, who lives and grows and is always being itself, without ever any need of approval, was the only thing in this world I could see as offering the example and support I was so desperate for.

Outside of the reality of my personal needs, the experience being shared between me and Trystan in the warm, softly lit ambiance of the living room was still mutually private, and apart from the music on the stereo, silent. We had connected periodically, but not since my distraction from the tea and new investment in my personal hell. Earlier in the evening, we spoke of going out to the nearby park, and though I didn't want to disrespect his process, my fully immersive depression offered a powerful imperative for me to get the fuck out of that house and my arms around a tree. I reached out to engage him, doing my best to maintain composure, and offered the suggestion of a new direction, towards the park.

Unfortunately, Trystan and I were in very, very different spaces and he didn't really want to take a twenty-minute walk in negative fifteen degree Celsius weather. I did well to hold back my initial reaction to his desires, as everything inside of me wanted to blame him and lash out at him for being so selfish. How dare he not forfeit what was honest to him for what I needed in my challenges?! Didn't he know how upset I was? No, he didn't, and neither was it his responsibility to take care of me. It was mine. Only I could truly help myself in what I needed at that time; I knew that truth even when my ego tried to convince me that my challenges were somebody else's fault and responsibility.

Somehow, the realization of this personal responsibility offered a sense of courage, and so I decided I was going to hug a tree with or without him. Layering up for the weather took a bit of time, and just as I was about ready to leave, Trystan was open to coming outside with me, but not to the park. The furthest outside he was willing to go was to explore the birch tree on our front yard. I may have had this little boost of confidence that led me to preparing myself to leave solo, but I was still afraid and feeling utterly alone in my challenges. As such, the idea of forfeiting the park to enjoy the tree in our front yard seemed like a worthy compromise if it meant I'd have someone there with me.

We emerged onto our front deck from the soft yet personally suffocating warmth of the indoors. We stood there adjusting to the cold before we ventured to the tree a mere fifteen feet away. Just being outside and knowing that I was moving towards what felt like my salvation almost immediately helped me calm down. After a few minutes of acclimatizing to the cold, we went over to the tree and each took a turn hugging it. The sense of relief that came from embracing this honest expression of natural life was noticeable, but not by any means a solution to my challenges. Back on the porch, conversation moved slowly between me and Trystan as the mutual privacy had been suspended for the moment. I took this opportunity to share what I was confronting inside myself. Trystan was much more internal than I was during this talk and I began to feel self-conscious. There was a noticeable worry that I was impeding on his experience by wanting to *language* mine. However, he shared space considerately and asked me some important questions to help me move through what I was facing.

At a point of silence between us, I was standing on the porch looking out onto the snowy yard, watching the patterns from the streetlight transform as they passed through the bare branches of the birch tree. Seemingly spontaneously but perfectly timed, Trystan broke the silence with a poignancy that would direct the rest of my night:* "James, I see you as a guy who really likes to have control."

With a subtle sense of self-defeated acceptance, I immediately responded, "Ha, yeah."

Once we returned to the warmth of the indoors, the depth of legitimacy of Trystan's comment echoed through my self-awareness and began to manifest as potent emotions. My earlier challenges of feeling self-alienated and responsible for my depression prevailed, and the further distressing implications of Trystan's observations only served to exacerbate them. Yet, for some reason, there was still this added sense of self-confidence, of competence in being able to navigate my way through this experience independently. I remembered the importance of

---

* It has become a trend that Trystan's poignant comments tend to awaken deep internal processing for me, within and without the psychedelic experience. Personally, I would speak to this as being a favourable expression of his wisdom.

surrendering to the honesty of my emotional experience and letting the process of cathartic exploration direct me towards successful integration and healing. It seemed clear that an ongoing neuroticism of control was somehow perpetuating the psychological patterns I was playing out to create my depression. It also seemed clear that in order for me to push through these patterns and find new direction in myself, I needed to go deeper into the dark emotional source of these patterns. I needed to work with the increased emotional potency unlocked by the mushrooms to dive into the root of my issues and beyond. I needed to release all rational control of myself, completely surrender to my darkness, and allow it to move me in whatever way was most honest.

With this realization, I also had the discerning awareness of there being other people in the space who would likely be affected by my behaviour. Sia, aware that Trystan and I were on mushrooms, was now home and painting at the dining room table. I told Sia and Trystan that I was entering a strange space and asked if they were comfortable with me flailing and acting strange for a little while. Thankfully, they encouraged me to go through my process however I needed to, and so began my express route to madness.

It started as throwing around my clothes as I took off my outdoor gear. It seemed like doing so was the most accessible expression of non-control available in the moment, yet this was only the beginning. I eventually went into my room and started pacing around erratically. As I furthered my surrender, the emotional and physical process unfolding manifested as new thought patterns and perspectives on myself. It was so obvious; I was attempting to exercise militant control over myself in almost every element of my life, constantly directing what I was thinking or saying, the way I moved, the things I did with my day, and the foods I ate. Yet this often came with a sense of failure that left me punishing myself and pushing this attempt at control even harder as my life unfolded. I was never allowing myself to just be myself and was constantly self-punishing for it. The expansive influence this neuroticism of personal expectations for self-control and the effect that failing to meet them was having over my entire life was disheartening. So much of my personal issues at the time, and likely of most of my life, were expressions of this pattern playing out over and over again. If I was to address the symptoms of this pattern, I had to release it at its root. I needed to release all control over myself and let the energy I had been blocking through this self-control to process.

This next stage in my journey was going to be very dark. I knew this intimate darkness looming over me was not going to be pleasant and didn't want it to affect the energetic environment of the communal space. In my last expression of personal control before completely releasing into madness, I picked up my thrown clothes from the living room and returned to my bedroom for some privacy. It is difficult to explain how I did this, but alone in my room, I opened the floodgates of my psyche and let it all pour out.

Moving around in an extremely awkward dynamic of physical gestures, I began to clean and tidy the space, in what I understand now to have been an externalized expression of an internal cleansing of my psyche. Very strange movements developed and I began spontaneously twitching and spasmodically changing directions. My mind was going crazy, nothing made any sense, and I made no attempt to make sense of anything. The emotional blockages that were perpetuating the patterns of personal self-degradation were emerging from my psyche and communicating through my physical body. Deep psychic tension, the culmination of who knows how long worth of self-repression and punishment, manifested as brief moments of tension and tremors across my entire body. I would freeze all my muscles and stand on up my toes like some severely autistic children do. Grunting and groaning as I felt my kinetic energy release out of me, my body would relax again, but only for a moment as I continued my journey through horrifyingly schizophrenic thoughts and disconcertingly capricious postures.

Still in the depths of a madness hitherto unfaced in myself, the irrational processes I was moving through began to transmute into a clear, yet still eccentric perspective on what was happening in myself. I could see my common actions, thoughts, feelings, lifestyle choices, relationships, and even social niche from the stance of a broader perspective. My mind was still adrift in lunacy, but the symptoms of mental illness I had been showing over the last couple of months were crystallizing into a valuable perspective, and I felt the need to record it so I could reflect on it later. Normally, I wouldn't try to write things down while I was facing the shadow with psilocybin, but this was unlike any journey I had ever faced and all my normal constructs of self-direction had been long since surrendered in favour of delirium. I honoured my intuitive call and began to help my process along with the technology of paper and graphite. Grabbing my sketchbook and pencil, I went back into the living room to mindmap *alienation* and its role in my life.*

Sitting in the middle of the hardwood floor in our open concept living space, the involuntary jerks and twitches, spontaneous groans, and expressions of tension continued. With my sketchbook in front of me and a pencil in hand, I wrote "alienation" in the centre of my page and things began to piece together. As the mindmap unfolded through me and onto the paper, it revealed that since my last mushroom journey, where I was shown that I had spread myself thin by over-investing myself in external and

---

* A mindmap is a written brainstorming technique done to help explore and connect various elements of a particular idea.

social responsibilities, I had established a lifestyle that alienated me from the outside world. I had created a pattern of spending so much of my time inside my home, stressing my creative process in an effort to complete a novel, that I was developing xenophobia.*

I refused offers to go out and resisted anything that took me away from my house. When I did finally go out, usually bred of desperation for human connection, I felt uncomfortable and unfamiliar with how to interact with people, which only furthered the justification to stay inside.

The symptoms of this vicious cycle were far more expansive than just my xenophobia. It was clear that I had also developed an overwhelming fear of germs and infectious diseases, embodying strange control tendencies that affected my relationships with others. I was losing track of my equity and finances and developing a general mistrust of other people. All the major and peripheral symptoms of mental illness seemed to stem from and exacerbate the same root issue: I had lost sight of the purpose and passion that previously fuelled me in life. In the effort to focus on writing, my passion, I had lost sight of the purpose *behind* my writing and replaced it with a cultivated state of constant confusion, desperation, and depression. It was that sense of purpose I had cultivated over the previous few years that had always helped me feel grounded and grateful for what I do, and I had allowed it to slip away.

Staring at the mindmap drawn out in front of me, I twitched, grunted, and tremored. My head was spinning and my awareness was catapulted through the dark emotional recesses of my mind. Even with the granted perspective on what was creating my challenges, I was buried in the immersive awe of a seemingly endless expanse of psychedelic terrain. The geometric rendering of the psilocybin metabolizing in my body still painted my

---

* A fear of strangers.

awareness with complex fractals, my body was still awake with energetic sensations of a contorted and uncomfortable nature, and my mind felt erratic and unstable. With the added intensity of realizing how deeply I had pushed myself into depression in such a short period of time, the experiential characteristics of this journey felt like looking down the barrel of insanity.

That's when the next realization came into light—something far more terrifying than seeing myself as the source of my own depression. In the process of having released control of myself, in the hopes of finding solace from mental instability, I accessed a realm of madness inside of me. I had opened a door inside of myself, the living expression of which could best be described as a psychotic episode. This process offered me a clearer perspective of myself and the psychospiritual challenges I was facing, but it was unlike anything I had ever experienced with mushrooms up to that point. The anomalous state of awareness it unlocked was exponentially more unsettling than the depression it sought to dispel. A voice inside me, one that I have since learned to trust in the depths of terror, clearly stated, "James, be careful. You've never been this deep before and you don't know how to get out of it or if you even can."

Have I gone too far? How the hell do I come back from this?

I thought briefly about the situation I was in, unsure of what to do. Though I was frozen in the infinite moment of 'now,' encased in fear of having broken my brain, a spark of hopeful insight emerged. If mindmapping *alienation* brought me perspective on how I got to where I was, perhaps mapping *healing* would help me find my way back to normality. Flipping over to a new page in my sketchbook, I wrote "healing" in the centre and began to meditate on it. The same uncomfortable and perceivably schizophrenic body tremors and spasms continued unfazed, but the *feeling tone* associated to them shifted. The whole process remained painful, but the information emerging was different. At first, what started to come through me was scattered and conceptually asymmetrical, but as I drew it out, the message became clear:

> *Through the unfathomable diversity of potentials in human experience, I saw underlying patterns of emotionality. We all face challenges of relative suffering and most of us are lost in the struggle to prevail through it. I am not alone; we are not alone. Pain and challenge are part of the archetypal darkness fundamentally present in the collective consciousness, opening itself through each of us, opening itself to be seen. It comes through us as an opportunity to learn our true strength to persevere and bring forth the archetypal light of healing and gratitude into existence. The emergence of darkness is an opportunity for us to find ourselves capable of shining light. This darkness is painful, but sometimes healing feels like hurting.*

I knew that this perspective was far from a solution to the plight of human existence as it plays out on the global scale, but on a personal level it offered me some solace. Yet, the painfulness of the process wasn't subsiding. It was actually becoming denser. My body was no longer twitching, but seizing up as all my muscles went hard and I could feel my organs compressing inside of me. Compounding on top of this physical compression was an energetic tension that not only completely infiltrated me but even spread out around me like a cloud of agony. I was absolutely overwhelmed and didn't know what to do. I was lost, alone, and living a hurt beyond anything previously fathomable. Then something snapped in me and inside my mind I cried out, "I'm sorry, I don't know what to do, please help me, please!"

All of a sudden, without forethought, I threw myself down

to the floor fiercely, flat across my belly, and brought my knees and hands up behind me as if they were tied together behind my back. With my eyes closed, I rode the metaphorical thought of the psychedelic experience into my own personal mythos. I was now on the chopping block atop an Aztec pyramid, about to be sacrificed. I could see elaborate patterns of geometry woven between Mayan glyphs as I felt my head pulled back by my hair and a knife glide deeply across my throat. I felt the energetic tension intensify with the unmistakably distinct sensation of bleeding to death from my throat while the elaborate patterns in my vision became increasingly violent and confusing. Harder, deeper, fuller—the sensation of dying reached a crescendo that seemed to freeze time in a place of total density, and then, release. The tension, the grunting, the spasms, the confusion, the fear, the pain were gone, all of it. The only things left in my awareness were beautiful patterns, solace, and a sense of gratitude that felt like having made it home to the heart of God.

It hurts most just before release was the first thought to come as I returned from pure awareness and back into a relative context. When I realized and accepted my helplessness and opened myself to personal humility, I released the walls of assumption and assertive independence. Crying out earnestly for help inside of myself and surrendering to the acceptance that no, I didn't really know what to do, was that which opened me to the help I needed all along. This was a personal process, but I saw a human commonality in it. I saw that when overwhelmed by the wrath of facing the darkness of oneself, it is in *surrender* to the emotional honesty of humility in our humanness that we can access our inner wisdom and an encompassing dimension of support.

The darkness will come no matter what we do; it is sown into the very fabric of human existence. Yet, if we are able to *surrender* the honesty of our emotional challenges and accept that no, we don't always know what to do about it, eventually we will be offered exactly what we need to heal, though it will likely hurt more before it starts to feel better. It is those moments in life that offer us the most vital growth. Like stones being tumbled to a polish, eventually, we may tumble to a point of being able to shine. And then, in simply being ourselves as an expression of growth through personal challenge, we can become a beacon for those who are still lost in the dark.

I was still lying on my belly in the living room, relaxed and tender. Returning more and more into my body, I began to check in with myself. I felt shaken, but comparatively stable. Hindsight offers me the realization that what I had just gone through was a personal process of facing common human archetypes, but given my ongoing identification to the concept of '2012' at the time, it manifested in Mayan symbolism and I amplified the scope of my experiences to be clear signs towards that experience as having something to do with the supposed 'great shift' underway.

Arlo was also home at this point and he and Sia were in the living room throughout the course of my disturbingly powerful series of moments. They would later tell me that they could see that I was in a very dark state of mind and were holding me in a place of love and support, but also giving me the space to go through whatever it was I was going through. In the moment, however, I felt as though my energy was making them uncomfortable, so I left to go connect with Trystan, who was downstairs in his room.

I had just travelled through an experience of being a religious sacrifice atop an Aztec pyramid in the midst of facing what I felt was the permanent fracturing of my psyche, the profundity of which I identified as being part of some grander transpersonal process the planet was undergoing (which it may or may not have been). I felt healed in a way, but also shaken and moved by an imperative to 'do something.' I had no idea what this *something* was, but figured Trystan would have some perspective on the whole thing.

Managing my way through the light-headedness and lack of balance echoing from the energetic storm I had just weathered, I made it to the basement. Trystan's door was open and as soon as I walked into his doorway, he turned to me, asking, "What the fuck is going on?"

"I don't know but it's intense," I replied.

"No shit."

We discussed what each of us had been going through and it became clear that we had almost exactly polar opposite experiences. I had been going through deeply personal emotional healing, and he had been getting intense messages from what felt like higher dimensional, alien intelligences. We tried to hash out what we each had learned in our personal experience in the hope to make sense of what was happening to us. We also had the mutual intention to discover that there were underlying planetary patterns that were influencing our experiences as a part of the 'great 2012 shift.'

The exact details of what we talked about in that heightened state are loose in my memory now, but it is clear that we didn't find enough correlation between our experiences to support a planetary influence, regardless of how much we tried to piece them together with a confirmation bias. It seemed as though our established hypothesis regarding the experience's source as being within an evolution of planetary consciousness was not as solid as we wanted it to be. This was a strong bit of evidence that perhaps my assumptions, based on the New Age belief structure regarding 2012, may not have held the basis of truth I deeply wanted them to given the sad state of human affairs on the planet.

With a mild sense of disappointment in not finding reason to believe that we had just tapped some energetic vein of planetary transcendence, there was still perceivable value in the process of talking our experiences out with each other. The conversation offered me a perspective on the concept of balance and how I had created an imbalance in myself. After being shown that I wasn't investing enough time into my creative projects, I swung the pendulum too far in the opposite direction in an effort to self-correct. In doing so, I had isolated myself so deeply from the outside world—only working within myself and on my personal projects—that I had lost sight of my purpose: a balance between doing my personal work and embodying my skills outwards into the world.

If I was to create psychological balance while still playing my inner hermit to work on personal creative projects, I needed to also send energy out into the social sphere around me to nourish my sense of social inclusion. If I didn't give a balance of energy to each, I would create a deficit in myself that would eventually manifest as mental instability. It was evident that I needed to continue to work on my book and stay committed to my writing, but I also needed to focus on the elements of my personal skills that functioned as social offerings, which at the time was event organization through a local group called Evolver Calgary.

Another element that came to light was my intention to foster personal success through entrepreneur-ship and self-publication. This required not only a commitment to the process of writing, but the building and cultivation of the cultural niche that would support me in blossoming into a successful professional. The niche that I built also had to feed back into the social substrate that offered me growth by providing something of value to those supporting me. If I was to make a career out of inspiring others through my inspired creativity, it was vitally important that I remained honest, grateful, and always mindful of returning value. That was the responsibility of artistic success, and if I failed to embody it, I would be merely living a game of egoic self-grandeur.

It was this that offered me the 'something' I needed to do, and the urgent imperative I travelled into my basement with quelled a bit when I saw it was a progressive 'something' rather than an immediate one.

Sitting downstairs, stretching in Trystan's room, I finally felt as though I had come out the other end of my psychotic episode and was heading back to baseline. It would unfold over the next few days that my depression had lifted, but in that moment, it was difficult to comprehend, as the intensity of my experience left me in a very raw state.

Ready to be grounded and come back to our sober selves, Trystan and I returned upstairs to share the space with Sia and Arlo. Together, the four of us drank soft ginger tea and ate snacks. I knew then and know now that the three of them were more than just my housemates. They were my family and I felt comfortable sharing anything with them, and so I did. I spoke honestly about my budding mental illness and that I had been starving myself of loving human interaction. I told them why I thought I was in that space, what I thought I needed to heal myself, and that I was still sensitive. I wanted them to know the context of my challenges so that they would know how to support me. If I was struggling and they didn't know that, it would be easy for us to misconstrue each other's intentions and create unneeded conflict. Their response brought me to tears when they swarmed me with a big group hug, letting me know that they loved me and would always be there for me.

In gratitude, we shared the rest of the evening together, listening to music and talking about the experiences we had all been confronting, both the hurting and the healing. That was when the correlations Trystan and I were searching for in the basement started to emerge more readily, as a synchronicity between the events of our lives and the personal psychospiritual processes each of us were facing surfaced. Regardless of whether or not this had anything to do with 2012, the cultural concept of it became the framework through which we integrated the implications of this synchronicity.

This is where things get odd, because I could very well just rationalize now that the correlations we made were a determination fallacy as we all wanted to believe in 2012, but what happened the next night is tough to toss away as a simple fallacy bred of desiring a specific logical correlation.

My sleep was deep when I went to bed that night, my dreams potent, and I woke refreshed. There is something about going through a deeply challenging psilocybin experience and facing the potency of my darkness that leaves me feeling lighter and fuller than before. I woke up with an awareness of gratitude for my night as I reflected on having been given everything I asked for on this journey: "perspective on my low-density energy, healing from whatever wounds this is sourced in, and some direction in moving forward."

I spent that day herb hunting through Chinatown with Trystan and discussing our experiences. Later that night, I ended up going out to see Kaminanda, a psychedelic electronic musician, play a show at a venue called The AREA. Throughout my night, almost every person I interacted with, often without cue from me, expressed having recently faced similar challenges to what I had just processed or harmonized directly with my vocalized experience of self-alienation. Repeatedly, those who I opened up to related that they too had just come to similar realizations about healing through their challenges.

My experiences during that following day and conversations of that night confirmed what I felt during my mindmapping session for *healing*: we are all in this together, and many of us are lost in the same way. Harvesting the fruit of releasing my xenophobia and embracing social community, I opened to experience what seemed like the transpersonal unfolding of a powerfully transformative process in myself and the people around me.

That night at the Kaminanda show, I had one of the most beautifully healing dances in recent memory. It was as if the music was rippling through my skin. I felt the barriers between myself, the music, and my dance dissolve away and each became reflections of each other into one infinite present moment, beaming with life, and I came to an epiphany that led me to writing the following later that night:

Our collective consciousness is transforming in a manner that is allowing us a direct realization of a wider spectrum of reality. Through each of us, we are unlocking a perception founded on the lateral connections of an ever-unfolding synchronistic whole. A perception that transcends our current level of consciousness— which can only understand time as a linear progression of past towards future—and as it blooms, it is experienced as what we call synchronicity.

There is something grander happening here than just us, yet by simply participating in our own transformation we are morphogenetically changing the reality we operate through into a divine realization of the interconnectedness between us— physically, psychologically, socially, energetically, emotionally. We are participating in a collective, synchronistic unfolding transformation into the now, the only moment that ever was and the moment we are coming to understand as the place where our journey begins, ends, becomes, and undoes. It's happening. Keep watch and remember: you're not the only one; look out upon each other in honesty and acceptance; we are all going through this together; we can help each other along the way towards now.

You are perfectly in line, on time, and loved.
Have trust, have faith, stay honest
And don't be afraid to accept help.
We are all in this together.
Re-member that.

Integration

Over the following days and weeks, I gradually noticed that the depression I had been facing was gone. In addition, the sense of being interconnected in a planetary process of personal awakening prevailed, and for the most part, continues to. The night of the supposed 'great shift of 2012,' the days leading up to it, and the days following, were indescribably nourishing. For me, there was no fear for the potential destruction of the planet or anything in that regard; I had only a sense of faith in humankind and love for the community that includes me—two things in which I am grateful to have learned to believe.

I look back at that time in my life and can see the attempts being made in myself, and in the people around me, to create a logical justification to there being empirical evidence for a pleasurable idea: that in some way we were all going to spontaneously awaken and manifest a more beautiful world. We all wanted this to be true. Why wouldn't we?

I can see now that many of the ideas being proposed in the larger cultural concept of 2012 were quite a stretch of the imagination (e.g., 'spontaneous ascension into fifth dimensional light beings'). But in their absurdity we are offered an opportunity to come back to a middle ground in our ontological perspectives, having explored what it might look like if we break the boundaries of personal potential embedded through the conditioning of conventional society. Here in 2015, it seems clear to me that the importance we associated to 2012 acted as a point for the human mind to place the personal and cultural *meaningfulness* of transformation.

I also see that 2012, the cultural meme, in many ways offered exactly what we wanted it to—positive change in many people and thus society in general. The new perspectives, releases of investment, worries, dramatic choices, and philosophies of

2012 that burgeoned in the cultural mind as a response to this meme pushed an imperative of exploring what it means to be oneself and to what degree of connection there may be beyond the individual. This, as a psychological reference point, created a set of experiences that allowed for that exploration to seat into the identity of many I know, and in turn, the cultural interactions and institutions they, and we, create with our actions, thoughts, and feelings. With the coming and passing of December 21, 2012, this new identity construct could be freed of its linear time shell and allowed to go on and play out in the lives of those who chose to maintain it.

The proliferation of the 2012 meme amongst an impressionable culture of spiritually minded, socially conscious, and proactively creative people opened a large-scale discourse on the concept of a transpersonal connection between humanity, the planet, and the cosmos, as well as what it means to live life to its fullest. That may have created space for many escapist ideals, but also created an arena for us to practice what it means to culturally navigate the implications such a connection has on our interpersonal relationships; a cultural navigation I feel, in time, will be of our great benefit.

As the book progresses through each smaller story,
the larger story,
that of the author themselves,
expands.

FACING FORGIVENESS;
EMBRACING THE SHADOW

The Spiralling Pattern

My relationship to psilocybin transforms along with me as I pass through stages of progressive maturity and self-awareness. Each time I step into the reality the mushrooms unlock from my mind, I find a slightly different 'me' reflected in the tryptamine mirror. This story, the one that concludes this trilogy, comes from an era in my practice when there was a limited set of reasons that would inspire me to explore what this medicine has to offer; not because I was attached to one method of usage or another, but because I had found the role it played most effectively for me at that time.

One of those limited reasons, the one that led me down the rabbit hole we are about to consecrate into literature, was coming to recognize myself as depressed. I don't mean 'sad' or just feeling down, but depression. It is a state of being that seems to slowly creep until it hits a tipping point and then, without warning, I am totally encompassed in a grey, flat world, engulfed by monotonous melancholy and morose mental-emotional patterns. This doesn't happen to me often, but I, like every human, am not totally free of its powerful reach.

Everyone goes through periods of depression in life; it is natural and beautiful in a painfully paradoxical sort of way. But when one is fully immersed in the experience, a higher understanding of this paradox is far from conceptual reach and it's very difficult to embody a sense of self-compassion or appreciation for its exquisite agony. But, I suppose that if it were possible to maintain that sense in the midst of depression, chances are none of us would really be all that depressed for very long.

A tendency I have observed in myself has been to try and 'fix' my impending depression 'problem' as soon as I recognize it beginning to grow within me. As it progresses, I eventually realize there's nothing I can do or fix, and all my attempts are futile. This causes me to feel defeated and I get upset with myself for being helpless, an emotional failure because I couldn't 'fix' my darkness. Being upset with myself in addition to already being generally depressed hinders my ability to do things that would probably help me feel better (like achieving simple daily goals), which further exacerbates the whole situation. As I get increasingly more depressed, I get less and less likely to desire interacting with others because I don't feel good about who I am, and this lack of social support further plays into my inner struggle. The situation ends up perpetuating itself through a downward spiral of deleterious behaviours that is incredibly difficult to break free from.[*]

I have learned that if I am mindful of my emotions and express them in a healthy way, I can, for the most part, evade this spiral before it begins, or at the very least, mitigate its intensity. I am able to allow my emerging darkness to pass through me with relative ease by letting go of there being a 'problem' with feeling down. I find solace when I release the desire to feel happy and simply embrace these emotions, while continuing to participate in a healthy and supportive social setting.[*] But of course, regardless

---

[*] This spiralling pattern is one I believe others face as well and can deepen to influence a person's mental health until depression hits a point far more suffocating than the average person will ever face. For those who haven't been there, it can be difficult to understand what this feels like and that once one is encompassed in this spiral, their entire life feels like it has fallen into a monstrous pit of personal despair without any perceivable escape.

of what I may understand about my dark emotions and how to navigate them, I am still subject to falling into the spiral. I am not exempt from being thrown by the waves of life. Thankfully, my bouts of depression have been relatively short-lived and gentle, but there have been a few periods in my life where 'gentle' has been the antonym to what I experienced.

Depression is cumulative, incubating and lying in wait beneath the surface of awareness until events in our present lives may trigger and awaken it within us. I see this culmination as being sourced in a history of trauma, embedded deep within the psyche. Likely formed in early life, trauma develops over the years in a manner wherein the emotional charge of the initial trauma and the defense mechanisms employed by the ego to protect the self from the wound (or wounds) accrued from that trauma repeat and reinforce themselves in one's personality. The behavioural patterns surrounding the ego's defense mechanisms develop as the total emotional charge associated to the initial trauma cumulates with experiences of similar emotions. With enough cumulative strength, these patterns take their stronghold as highly complex and destructive self-identify constructs.[†] These patterns and traumas are subconscious, and when one's personality becomes attuned to these emotional characteristics and perceived character traits, the resulting effects can be extremely difficult to release as they become the very substrate of one's whole life.[‡] This is especially challenging for those living in the often cold and disconnected

---

* I recognize how lucky I am to be able to have the mindfulness and sense of social support that allows for this.

† For example, self-repression, belief of oneself as unworthy of love, abandoned or inadequate, chronic anger or violence, self-deprecation, and emotional evasion, among other things.

‡ As a caveat, I am not a psychologist or a doctor. These are simply observations drawn from independent study and synthesized with personal experience. Depression is a complex disorder and I know I don't have the full picture.

society of the conventional Western world.

Due to the nature of Western society (emotionally repressive, mechanical, and psychospiritually adolescent, at best), most of us are bred into an ongoing state of emotional repression. Because of this, most of us never fully face the uncomfortable or dark emotional processes (wounds) that are ongoing in the psyche and subconsciously influencing the personality we autonomically express. Yet when these dark feelings are evaded or repressed, consciously or not, their ability to influence and direct our surface experience of life in a negative way becomes stronger. When this happens, these unacknowledged elements of ourselves degenerate the emotional dynamics of how we interact both interpersonally (the world perceivably outside of ourselves, such as other people) and intrapersonally (inwardly with ourselves, such as self-talk and self-image). These unfortunately common systems of unhealthy emotional processing manifest through one's personality in a wide variety of ways, including the disorder of depression.

I have come to realize, through studying psychology and exploring my emotions with psychedelics and meditative practice, that if I am in a state of depression, I have tapped into some pattern of wounding in my psyche (likely sourced in childhood trauma), heavily manifesting in the moment due to having been catalyzed by some recent or current event or set of events that brought out similar emotions. Furthermore, the level of depression I am experiencing is influenced by how directly the associated emotional charge of the current or recent events correspond to those patterns of trauma or wounding within my psyche; if the emotions and ego defense mechanisms subconsciously employed to deal with those emotions in the current event are the same as the emotions and mechanisms in a prevailing pattern of wounding, they will compound and the present experience will manifest with the cumulative charge of the entire history of that wounding.

Thus, the more pervasive and enveloping the depression, the deeper the manifest emotional charge and wounding patterns associated to the current or recent events embed themselves into my sense of self and personal history. When it's looked at this way, depression offers a great opportunity for me to tap into some deeply repressed emotions and heal some obviously influential patterns of trauma within myself.

But this is extremely difficult. The more potent the mafestation of emotional pain, the stronger the ego's defense mechanisms will become to protect me from the history of that trauma. I end up in a state of awareness where I am depressed and know that it's because I am not allowing myself to wholly feel the fullness of what is going on inside of me and thus am not understanding how to hold self-compassion and open a space to heal. But at the same time, my ego's defenses, protecting me from the deep-seated trauma in my psyche, are so strong that I am not able to go into those emotions because the ego will hijack any attempt to evade its defenses. I end up stuck in surface-level emotions, reacting to the depression rather than exploring the source of it. This is where a psychologist would come in handy. They could use *language* mechanisms to coerce and manipulate me into some type of catharsis through creating a psychological feedback loop between us. Ideally it would look something like this: they ask me a question, I answer, they read the subtle triggers 'between the lines' of what I am saying, they ask me another question, I come to some realization and cry, they support me, I release and maybe heal. But, I don't have a psychologist. Partially, because I don't have enough money to be supported by a professional. But also because I don't really believe that our conventional institutions have trained psychologists that I could trust enough to really allow them to 'open' me.

This is where the mushrooms come in for me. I have found that they are able to bring down my ego's defenses and open the floodgates of my emotions. This helps to push me into the cathartic release I need while exploring the wounds, memories, and triggers connected to my negative state of being. Cultivating this type of experience has offered me the emotional release and perspective on myself needed to surpass whatever phase of depression I may be in.*

This is by no means a pleasant or safe practice, nor would I encourage anyone to try it, but it has worked for me. As I mentioned earlier, I have not faced deep and pervading depression very often in my life, but the story I am about to tell you describes one of those times and what it took to pass through it.

Point Of Departure

I had recently fallen deeply in love with a woman. She and I had entered places of vulnerability and intimacy that were, in many ways, very new for both of us. We had been seeing each other for several months when she 'came clean' with me about something she had been withholding, something she had even looked me in the eyes and outright lied to me about. Out of respect to her, I will not explain what this something was, but will offer to you that what it brought up for me were the emotional archetypes of betrayal, loneliness, shame, and guilt.

At the point in our relationship when the confession was brought forth, we had only just come to fully recognize the depth of intimacy we were experiencing and the love growing between us. With the truth of lies told brought to mutual light,

---

* There is also fantastic evidence that the active alkaloid in mushrooms, psilocybin, may actually create a neurological change in people with chronic depression that reduces the overactivity in areas associated to chronic depression. For more information, look up the research of Prof. David Nutt and Dr. Robin Carhart-Harris.

I had to decide whether or not I wanted to continue to be in a relationship with her.

Can I continue to offer her honest trust after it has been so violated?

The days following her confession were consumed by this question. Honestly, I could relate to what drove her to make the choices that she did. I understood what must have influenced her to lie to someone she loved, how hard it must have been to be honest with me after how long this lie was ongoing, and how potent the implications surrounding the whole situation were. But even with this ability to relate, I was deeply hurt, and the most vital element of an intimate relationship and the hardest to rebuild once burned—the ability to trust—was called into question.

In the exploration of what this context of challenges meant to me as a person and to our relationship, it became pretty clear that regardless of the hurt I was experiencing, I was still in love with her. Somehow her offering of truth, even though it was likely bred of having hit a point where the lies either needed to expand or to be dissolved, offered me a sense of being able to trust her; it must have been so hard for her to be honest with me. Inspired by love, I decided that I wanted to stay together and offer her the opportunity to make right on those poor choices and continue to build on the beauty we were discovering in each other.* I wanted to be with her, to share and explore in vulnerability and intimacy. Maybe this was a decision made out of desperateness for love, but I don't regret it. The moment I told her "I forgive you. I want to be with you. I love you," sitting on the boulevard across from my

---

* Little did I know that we would both play into a dynamic where that pattern of lying, withholding truth, and generating betrayal would later be repeated at the cost of our relationship—but that's another story.

house, her arms flying around me with so much force that we both went down to the grass, kissing and crying together, will stay with me forever.

Things on the surface between us had been addressed, and we were ready to move on with our relationship. But the subconscious implications of the gravity of this lie began to have a very deleterious effect on my life.

Over the next few days, I began to feel constantly angry, uncomfortable in my own skin, shameful, sad, and scared. I knew this wasn't at her or because of her; it was mine, 'for me' and 'of me.' The implications were settling in and bringing me deep into a dark, depressed state. When I would wake in the morning, an all-encompassing sense of life being grey, and flat, and simply awful in every way would arise and grow as my day continued. Of course, this was negatively affecting my quality of work, focus, and creativity, in addition to my relationship with her, my household, my friends, and the quality of my life in general. Nothing beamed with the sparkle of 'special' and I was moving through a world of darkness without a horizon upon which to find light. It only took a few days to emerge, but this was maybe the deepest sense of depression and emotional anguish I had ever faced; I was locked into the downward spiral.

As I discussed earlier, I was aware that there were deeply-seated emotions that I needed to release if I was to find solace in this challenge, but I was cold and dry. The only emotions that I could access were the symptoms of depression, not the source. I was closed off from what was happening inside of myself because I was blinded by my ego's defenses: projections of blame, inability to look deeper than the most recent catalyzing events or focus on my feelings, confusion, self-deprecation patterns applied against my depression itself, anger, and frustration at myself for 'failing' at being a healthy human, among other things. These were all responses to the effects of depression, not the source emotions I needed to explore, but again, I was trapped in them.

I was lost within self-perpetuating patterns of defeat and anguish in a way that I hadn't experienced since returning home from my travels in Australia and living in my parents' basement, hiding the fact that I felt psychotic from substance abuse. And even that experience didn't feel as heavy as this one.

In the midst of all of this, it was clear to me that I had tapped a very deep pattern of wounding in my psyche. Yet, I was completely locked out of its source by the incessant defensiveness of my ego. I couldn't continue to live that way and there seemed to be no escape without help. So, I decided that I needed to bypass my ego and open the floodgates of my emotional self, to eat three and a half grams of dried psilocybin mushrooms with the intention of exploring my wounds. Hopefully, this would open a space for me to release the strong repression that was negatively influencing my healing process. But this darkness I was facing was powerful, and just eating the mushrooms didn't feel like enough. The journey I was going to take couldn't allow for any influence other than my inner-self, my wounds. I needed to create a setting for this journey where the physical darkness would match the depth of emotional darkness I was facing. I needed to ensure I accessed the release I needed and there was only one way I could think of to ensure this. I would take my mushroom journey in a sensory isolation tank.

Towards the Tank

Throughout my teenage years, my best friend was a guy named Josh. He was a movie guru with an impeccable taste in strange, potent films. Chronically ill throughout most of his childhood, he spent a lot of time in his room watching movies and making art. He is now an accomplished artist and painter. Josh is a few years older than me and so his prime movie-watching days were during the 1980s, the golden era of animatronics, strange storylines, and pushing social boundaries. Unlike myself, a sheltered child being raised by rural Newfoundlander Christians with a strong investment in their 'moral value' belief systems, Josh had the ability to watch whatever he chose without much parental censorship. So, when he and I started to become good friends during my age of rebellion, he helped guide me in and through the coolest films in his repertoire. Slowly but surely, and with the help of copious amounts of cannabis and the companionship of another great teenage friend, Andy, the three of us managed to watch pretty much every film my parents ever censored from me and far more.

It was in those years that I was exposed to the film *Altered States*. It starred William Hurt as an anthropologist with a radically similar last name to mine who was experimenting with sacred Mesoamerican visionary plants in a float tank.* The plot was loosely based around the work of John C. Lilly, an eccentric scientist who specialized in sensory isolation and dolphin communication, most famous in the counterculture for his self-experimentation with LSD in these tanks.

It might have been my being young and impressionable, or

---

* I hadn't made the radical connection between the content of that movie and the direction I would end up taking in my life until writing this story. I had seen this film long before I knew anything about psychedelic mushrooms.

maybe I was simply predisposed to being interested in exploring consciousness, but that film became one of my favourites. I watched it over and over again, embedding the characters into my identity, fantasizing about the opportunity to actually try one of these tanks. From sixteen to twenty-five years old this desire stayed with me, but no accessible opportunity to float ever presented itself.

Then, in some serendipitous social alignment, when I moved to Calgary in the autumn of 2010, I met a group of amazing people that would later invest in a personal tank. After nearly ten years of wanting to try one of these tanks out, I suddenly had one available for my experimentation at a friend's house just a few blocks away!

The tank was stored in a private residence that was acting as an unregistered healing centre. Affectionately called The Cove, it was advertised through word of mouth, and if you heard about it, you could book a float for yourself. The Cove, totally ahead of its time for Calgary, Alberta, ran exclusively on a 'gifting' business model: your float was a gift and you could voluntarily express gratitude for this gift in any way you chose (if you chose to at all), wherein monies were obviously welcomed but never insisted upon. The Cove operated over the course of a few years and played a major role in the cultivation of an entire community of floaters and like-minded people. It was a converging point for open discourse and self-exploration of many types. I had several powerful floats throughout the time that it operated, sober and otherwise, and the experience of floating had actually become seated in my higher-order identity constructs. Floating felt like a part of who I was, similar to the manner in which the psychedelic experience, meditation, and sexuality feel like a part of who I am.

At the time this story of depression and soon-to-be intense anguish shut inside a watery ego-grave takes place, The Cove was starting to disband. The property owners were ready to move these 'wide-eyed hippies' out of their house to likely be replaced by some Albertan expression of the nuclear family. The night I was to face this great challenge of depression would be my last ever float at The Cove.

Operation of floats at that time was being exclusively organized by one of the founding members of the house, Skye Dreamer, who is also a close brother of mine. Earlier in that month, I had been contacted by him and informed in advance as to the end date for all floats. Though it was very important to me that I took the opportunity to get into the tank once more, due to a constellation of other factors, I wasn't able to get organized and get over there. I had pushed the timeframe for this float so close to the deadline that I was actually going to be the last non-house member to float before its disassembly and relocation to a professional business venue.

Scheduling a float at The Cove usually included 'regular business hours' and a professional feel to the exchange, so being able to do this float late at night and high on psychedelics was by no means a standard. I had connected with Skye in advance and spoke to him about my intentions and desires, communicating its importance but not the full details of my situation. He generously agreed to support me in this journey and was willing to hang out at home that night to ensure that the tank was prepared for me and that I got in and out of it safely.* We arranged a time and I was written into the logbook to ensure there were no personal overlaps with any members of the house.

On the night of this float, I was, to say the least, pretty anxious about the whole thing. I may have taken many deep, painful journeys and in turn have always found myself out the other side stronger, healthier, and more courageous in general, but I was still intimidated by it. The potential calibre of this

---

* He has repeatedly shown this calibre of support to me and to others throughout the time I have known him, a beautiful expression of him as a person.

journey was a uniquely challenging one. I knew there was a swarm of darkness brewing beneath the surface of my mind and I was consciously choosing to unlock its painful uncertainty into my immediate reality. It's one thing to be prepared in case a psychedelic experience goes dark; it is a whole other thing altogether to know in advance that it is an all-consuming darkness you are intending to open.

My float was booked for 8:00 pm and so I started my brew a couple of hours earlier, timing it so that I would take my medicine at sundown and head towards the tank.

I prepared my dose, 3.5 dried grams, and took some time with the mushrooms before I started crafting them into a drink. I'm on the fence regarding whether or not these mushrooms have an essence of consciousness/spirit that exists as objective and independent of the human relationship to them. I have many experiences that offer me potential validation to their consciousness, but that perception is filtered through a human mind constantly projecting itself onto the world perceived as 'outside' in an effort to create a relativistic *meaningfulness* that supports the metaphorical substrata of self-identity of the behavioural patterns of the ego. What I am confident in is that whether or not the mushrooms' personality exists independently of the human relationship to them, speaking to the mushrooms in advance as if they were separate from me helps establish a psychological substrate for the upcoming experience. Speaking to them as if they were a teacher or a healer and playing into a personal myth by telling them my intentions and anxieties, as well as being fully expressive and honest with what has inspired me to connect with them helps me to establish my preferred mindset for the journey. It also allows me to create a psychological relationship with the mushroom experience based on reverence, which enables me to more completely *surrender* with trust that what I will be shown on a journey will be what I need to heal.

After a self-perpetuated counselling session with a handful of dried mushrooms, I began to prepare my dose into a drink. Eating the dried mushrooms or making a simple tea is a great way to engage them, though for me I have found pleasure in crafting different combinations of herbs, including the mushroom, to create a unique brew. Each different herb offers a qualitative difference in my experience, and in learning their independent effects, I can blend them together to craft a certain influence on my experience, such as potentiating the mushrooms, calming anxiety, or lessening digestive issues. This particular one was made by:

- First decocting reishi mushrooms for about an hour
- Adding the psilocybin mushrooms to gently simmer in the reishi decoction for an added 30 minutes
- Straining out all the stock for the decoction and adding it to a blender with:
  - Cacao paste
  - Cacao butter
  - Honey
  - He Shou Wu
  - Cayenne
  - MCT (medium chain triglycerides) oil
  - Salt
- Blending until frothy and drinking hot

Including reishi mushroom into my psychedelic sessions has shown to be beneficial for me on various levels. Most specially, the calibre of inner narrative they catalyze is very supportive and seemingly wise. The cacao and honey have been used with the mushroom in Mesoamerican tradition for a very, very long time. It covers their pungent flavour and offers a softening of the peripheral body stresses of being high, while also potentiating

88

their primary alkaloids by acting as an MAOi. The He Shou Wu is also an MAOi and supportive to the liver. The cayenne helps the uptake of the medicinal components of the drink. The MCT oil helps with nourishing the body while not eating throughout the duration of the trip, and the specific fat molecules in it also work as a type of 'brain fuel.' Salt balances out the flavours. Blending it all together alchemizes these separate components into a new thing that hadn't existed before: a thick, chocolatey psychedelic beverage, supportive on various levels of one's experience.

I drank my hot and foamy ticket to emotional release in my unlit living room. Sitting in front of the large windows that peered out across a nearby field, I watched daylight transform into dusk beyond the foreground of the street lamps. When it comes to mushrooms, I have learned that my preference is to have my dose/brew in one place, 'base camp,' and then physically journey to the place where I will explore the experience at its fullest, then return to base camp when I come down. The psychological pattern this establishes in the continuity of my mushroom ex-periences seems to reinforce the idea of being on a 'journey of exploration.' It also allows for whatever emotional disturbances I face in that journey to be left in the place they were released, rather than having my living room or bedroom house the residue of my expulsed emotions. This way, once released, they can be *fully* released rather than the pain of that experience itself logged into my normal habitat. And so upon finishing my drink, I bundled into my outdoor gear and began walking to The Cove.

With the sun down far enough that there remained no more residual light in the sky, night had only just come to its fullness. There are a few different routes I could have taken, but I chose the one that went through the nearby Confederation Park.* This

---

*This is the same park that has found its way into each of the experiences in this trilogy. It is a truly wonderful place to which I have attached many positive memories.

route took a bit longer, but the inspiration of being around trees while on psychedelics is unlike any other experience in life. This particular park had several beautifully large poplar trees that reached to the heavens along the path that took me to The Cove. Their size allowed them to stand out against the backdrop of the night sky and created the feeling tone of regality, and to reflect their potent confidence as expressions of unconditional presence before venturing alone into the tank felt like a vital ingredient to my journey.

Coming off the main road, a constantly busy and hectic strip, the mushrooms took their first breath as a sigh of relief to be entering the park. Walking through it, I felt gratitude for this sanctuary nuzzled in a valley with hills to block out the busy city around me. Slowly traversing along the trail, looking up at the trees to my right, the ability for the mushrooms to open the capacity to relate and empathize with the energetic characteristics of plants in general came to subtle awareness. Looking upon the powerfully tall poplars, I could feel their presence and age. It was inspiring, and though punctuality is not my greatest strength and I was already running late for my float, I stopped to honour my excitement and bear witness to this beauty as fully as possible. Standing still for the first time since I drank my chocolatey psychedelic drink, the mushrooms began to blossom a wonderfully pleasant anxiousness in my solar plexus. Enlivened by the energetic surges inside of me and my unlocked ability to directly experience the feeling tone of the natural environment around me, I was inspired to dance.

Mushrooms move me, literally, and when I release into intuitive movement with them, I seem to awaken an ability to draw geometric structures of a complex and fluid nature with the movement of my entire body. It is as if I am beginning to somatically express the fresh patterns of energy flowing through my psychophysiological system as the mushrooms alter my mental-emotional context and awaken a new *meaningfulness* of reality. These movements feel more like prayer than dance, but then again, what's the difference? Standing beneath those trees, staring up at them in awe as I danced, I could feel another dimension within the seemingly empty space that enveloped me. My dance wasn't just movement through space but an exchange of weight and momentum between my body moving through space and an otherworldly tactile dimension that somehow supported the space I was moving through, visually manifesting as geometric patterns in the air.

The mushrooms were definitely kicking in; I was fully immersed in this experience of motion. I felt called to stay in the park and explore my dance under and amongst the different trees. I wanted to allow the energetic exchange between myself and the unique energetic tone of each tree to open me up to new experiences of somatic expression. But, I also knew that it was this very inspiration that I was seeking to avoid when selecting the tank as my choice for the night. I knew that the darkness and the exploration of my depression was the larger intention for this evening, and that the brief break to dance was a blessing but also a distraction from the emotions I wanted to explore. With this understanding, I continued towards my destination.

Even though it was obvious to me that I had fully entered the psilocybin mindspace, there were no other people around me to relatively measure my level of disconnect from baseline, so contextually, I felt quite grounded. At least, that was until I walked into The Cove.

There were about five blocks between leaving the park and entering the house. I had no idea who would be home. The last time I came over for a float while on mushrooms, the entire living room was full of people playing board games, which was slightly awkward. So as I approached the house this time, I took a minute to check in with myself through a few internally focused questions:

How do I feel about entering the tank right now?
Afraid.
Is it the right decision to go through with this?
Yes.
How should I enter into the house?
With subtle confidence and honesty.

I walked up to the door and let myself in.

Now, one may not fully grasp the intensity of this next moment unless they have an idea of what The Cove looked like on the inside. This house was occupied by exquisitely creative, strange, fringe people, and its decor matched, to say the least. There were visionary designs, tapestries, plants, crystals, and installation art filling the living room space from floor to ceiling, hanging from the ceiling and everything in between; full, but not cluttered. The front door entered the living room area on the furthest back left corner. The aesthetically full living room extended to the right, where at the end of the wall was a large flat screen TV and in between was a welcoming setup of couches and a coffee table.

The front door opened to the left, leading the eye naturally to pan towards the back right end of the living room to see the flat screen TV and the visually immersive environment in between. As I stepped into the door, Skye was watching *The Avengers* through a (rather loud) 7.1 surround sound system. The scene I entered into was a close-up of some epic *Stargate*-like, mandalic, metallic blue machine activating and creating a deep and terrifying sound that rumbled through the whole space with an organ shaking bass tone.* I was, in the same moment, also taking in the extreme

---

* As in my kidneys, liver and large intestine.

fullness of every element in that space moving hallucinogenically, independent of everything around it but seemingly intermingled with the dynamics of the other independently moving elements of the room. At that point, I had become extremely aware of how very high I was, and the idea of getting into that tank got infinitely more intimidating.

Thankfully, Skye immediately paused the film when he saw me come in and gently walked over to welcome me with a soft hug and a warm sense of loving acceptance.

"Hey James. Welcome. How are you doing?" he asked.

"Well, I am just now realizing how incredibly high I am and feeling borderline overwhelmed by this space. Your energy is really grounding though, thanks," I responded.

He had a soft laugh with me and asked if I still wanted to get into the tank. I responded with a solid "yes" and he extended out his right arm, gesturing towards the steps into the basement.

"You know what you do from here. How long do you want to be in the tank for?"

"I don't know yet. If I'm not out in an hour and a half please come get me."

It was agreed and I went downstairs. It's part of the process to shower before getting into the tank, as it helps to keep the tank water clean. Typically, I would just get myself clean, but in this shower I was particularly mindful of preparing myself for what lay ahead. As I washed, I reminded myself why I was there and that I was capable of facing whatever may come. Once finished, without too much need to get dry, I simply wrapped a towel around me and headed into the float room.

The float room was a rather small space in the back end of the basement. It was basically large enough for the tank, a small walking space, and a very small area with a table and a chair. The tank took up the whole length of the room with enough space to reach from the tank to the light switch and towel rack against the opposite wall. The space with the chair was a slight alcove. The walls were a soft but deep blue and there were fake plants and vines hanging around, offering a less clinical feel. There was also some local visionary art on the walls and upon the aforementioned table sat a pleasant statuette, the shape of which I can't remember.

I have, as mentioned earlier, had many beautiful and transformative experiences inside this little room, and this was to be my last float within it. I took some time to appreciate the thick humidity of the air and the feeling tone of being in that room, a place where so many others had faced the literal darkness for transformation and release. I said hello to the tank and offered a small prayer to the waters inside of it. I was about to re-enter its womb and I knew the places I was about to go within myself were going to be dramatically unfamiliar. Like the mushroom, when entering into a relationship with something wherein the intention is that of healing or self-exploration, it is very helpful to engage this seemingly separate thing with a sense of humble appreciation and reverence to seed the quality of experience desired. I did this with the room, the tank, and the waters inside of it before I placed in my earplugs, turned out the light, entered the tank, closed the lid over me, and sealed my fate.

Round 1: Alien Landscapes

Navigating resistance to staying inside the tank and the repeated urge to get out is part of its journey. Similar to being resistant to stay sitting while in meditation, one chooses to acknowledge those feelings and then releases back into their meditation, or float in my situation. Usually, I could get at least thirty minutes into my float before I started to question whether or not I wanted to be inside the tank. This time, however, was not like any of my other experiences, even the other times I had been on mushrooms in there. As soon as the lid shut down on top of me, the presence of total sensory isolation immediately manifested as a complete sensory overload and I became distinctly aware of how poor of a decision this may have been.

Typically there are visions of some sort in my mushroom experiences, but I had not experienced anything like I did then with mushrooms. The sounds, colours, patterns, and sensations that were cascading through my awareness were completely overwhelming; it was closer to smoking a breakthrough dose of N,N-dimethyltryptamine (DMT) than any type of mushroom experience I knew of.

The tank had become a transport vessel for my consciousness. Immediately upon placing my body in its dark water, I was completely enmeshed into a totally alien mindscape. Not alien as in McKenna's 'Machine Elves' type aliens, but as in having the strong emotional character of being foreign and unfamiliar; so foreign and unfamiliar that it had the feeling tone of being inapprehensibly inhuman. It would be easy for my mind to attach the symbolism of 'the alien' to the emotional experience and for me to misunderstand the metaphor as ontologically real, but thankfully, I had already passed through that stage in my relationship to psychedelics. Otherwise, that initial awakening into the mushroom-augmented tank reality may have been even more terrifying.

There were geometric patterns that were infinitely unfolding, rippling, undulating, augmenting, germinating, enveloping, precipitating, flowering, evolving, involving, dissolving, and every other movement-describing '-ing' you can imagine and more. In fact, I might be incapable of describing it; theoretical wave mechanics might be the only form of language with the appropriate terminology. Regardless of words used, I was occupying what felt like a boundless field of visually rendered universal energy that permeated my entire being, sending echoes of complete bewilderment through it. But there was more than just vision in this place—there was this sound. I say "this sound" because it felt like only one sound, but a sound that was composed of every potential frequency within, above and below the audible range. It was an infinitely layered, asymmetrical, and non-repeating mechanical sound that seemed to be coming from every direction imaginable and even directions unimaginable and normally impossible.

It occurred to me that I had consciously chosen to place myself inside a watery coffin of psychedelic death and was now on the other side of existence, unsuccessfully trying to make sense of the topography of my experience. Typically, I choose a dose strong enough to break through into a total psilocybin experience, but not so much that I am incapacitated. This was too much. It was aesthetically enormous and almost completely non-functional to my intention of exploring personal wounds. Other than learning to muster the confidence it took to stay in the tank throughout such a perceptually challenging experience, I was achieving none of my intended goals with this medicine. I was told once that it was best to enter the tank after the peak was completed. Now I know why.

I had a platform of awareness that allowed me to understand that I could get out at any time, but I was committed to being in there for the duration. I was committed to facing what was emerging in the experience. Eventually, however, it was getting to be a bit too overwhelming and I began to question whether or not it was a responsible choice to keep submitting myself to such overwhelming stimuli.

Is this unhealthy for my mind?

Still, I felt committed to stay and face whatever challenges arose, and the idea of getting out seemed like an unbeneficial submission.

Within challenging psychedelic experiences, whether bred of deeply psychodynamic trauma or overwhelming aestheticism, having some conceptual and practical tools for navigating the experiences is vital. One tool that I have learned to help with anxiety within the tank experience is 'toning.' When the abundance of silence becomes too much and begins to feel as though it is closing in on me, breathing deep and sending out an audible sound representative of my current emotional state of being, progressing into a tone representative of the state I am seeking to enter is wonderfully beneficial. Within the tank, as the sound resonates inside the walls and bounces across the water, you can harmonize your voice to the various layers of echo, producing a concurrence of harmony. It can be a very soothing experience.

Thus, on the edge of submission to terror, I realized in a spontaneous moment of intuition that releasing my voice was what needed to happen. I was overwhelmed by these visions and alien sounds, and for the sake of my sanity inside that tank, I needed to enter myself into this space confidently in the only way I knew how. Beginning with a simple OM-type sound,* the echo bounced through the tank, washing over me, and I opened to feel more comfortable and expressed. As I sang, my sound began to evolve from simple tones to pop-star diva vibrato and a sense of self-confidence that shattered through my anxiety and brought the visions to a manageable place. It was as if my singing began to work like a feedback loop between my environment and the manifestations of my psychedelic mental-emotional states. It cancelled out the manifestations of an anxiety borne of bewilderment and the visions settled from an iron curtain of dread into a soft blanket of comfort and confidence.

In the exact moment I passed through to the other side of anxiety and found myself settled and ready to float, free of

---

* Like what spiritually invested yoga teachers get you to do before and after a class.

my non-functional, terrifying visions, I had a powerful, acute realization:

I need to pee, now.

I wasn't leaving the tank out of fear or resistance; I had overcome that challenge and was honouring my body, so I felt confident in taking my weightless form back into what was perceivably a gravitation field. Like a strange, coiled lizard person, I emerged from the tank, dripping wet and salty, and took the cold walk to the bathroom across the basement. Relieved on multiple levels and feeling ready to settle into the rest of my tank experience, I made my way as quickly as possible back to the humidity of the tank room and re-entered the indescribably inviting warmth of its dark water yet again. Shutting the lid above me, I fastened myself into what may hold as the most potent facing of the shadow I have ever encountered.

Round 2: Layers

After having mustered the sense of confidence I needed to traverse the alien mindscapes encroaching upon my sense of well-being, I felt like I could handle anything coming my way. I got back into that tank with a cavalier sense of being untouchable; this was a mistake. I feel that every time I enter a psychedelic experience holding the sense that my grandeur surpasses the power of the psychedelic I am going to take, I get humbled, hard. This experience was no exception.

The space inside the watery tank was substantially different this round. It was no longer a psychedelic playground of colors, it was the darkest (as in lacking perceivable photons) space I had ever been in and I felt totally isolated. The first emotional awareness that made itself present was the strong dull ache of a generalized fear and anxiety. Not an *acute fear* bred of being overwhelmed like when I first entered the tank, but a *chronic fear* echoing from deep inside of myself, sourced in some caliginous recess of my psyche. The surface manifestation of it came with the unsettling remembrance that I entered this experience because I was facing depression and wanted to address whatever emotional line of trauma was inspiring it. I knew in advance that this wasn't going to feel comfortable, but I hadn't really understood what the extreme context I had chosen for myself (being inside a float tank) would bring up from within me, the ramifications of which I was now coming to recognize.

The initial surfacing of dark emotions had an intellectualized explanation attached to it. I understood the feelings of being disconnected, alone, and scared about the lifelong implications of what had recently come up in exchange with my partner. It was seemingly clear that what I had needed to address these feelings was a friend to listen and hold a space of loving acceptance for me. But instead, I, for some reason unknown to me in that moment, decided it would be a better decision to do the exact opposite and enter a completely isolated space. And more so, not just enter it, but enter it on a strong dose of psychedelics.

The sense of claustrophobic loneliness that came with this realization was breathtaking. Literally, I gasped for air as every inch of my being was crawling with stress and screaming at me "get the fuck out of the tank you idiot, you're gonna hurt yourself." But I was invested (or maybe stubborn). I figured that if I was this afraid of what was going to come up from the tank, a physically safe space, then I must have accessed connection to an important trauma, deeply rooted inside of myself. Why else would the ego be so stark in its attempts to protect me from the impending emotions? I had tapped the vein of something strong and the accompanying emotional charge was powerful.

Stanislav Grof, a Czech research psychiatrist, might call what happened next in the experience as a psychodynamic emergence of a negative COEX system (system of condensed experience). A COEX system is a collection of seemingly separate memories orbiting around a root trauma from childhood (or birth trauma) that are all connected through a prevailing emotional theme and associated to specific psychological defense mechanisms. In a psychedelic session, he says that we can tap into these systems, wherein the culminated emotional charge of all the root trauma's associated memories emerge to the conscious awareness. We travel through increasingly deeper layers of memories associated to said COEX system until we access the root trauma in some way.

Regardless of whatever Grof may think about my experience or how he might describe it in psycholytic terms,* I had jumped into a river of negatively charged emotions and the psychedelic abundance of the mushroom experience was directing me towards inclement waters. I had two options: jump out and try to swim to shore and potentially find myself lost on the banks of unaddressed trauma, or hold fast to my inner strength and surrender to the turbulent flow with hope that the end result was a polish. I chose the latter and began to progress through the layers.

The next prominent set of associations to emerge were further connected to the emotional charge of loneliness, but more deeply expressed. I was alone in this tank when I knew that I needed the support one can only obtain through close friendship. I felt disconnected physically and emotionally from everyone, not just in the tank in that moment, but as a total cumulative charge of all loneliness I had ever faced manifesting as complete, holistic discon-nection. Each realization of disconnection progressed in intensity and in how broadly it affected the perception of my life as a whole.

I was away from my friends and had denied them access to

---

* A type of psychedelic-assisted psychotherapy.

support when they had offered it. I saw the disconnection with my romantic partner due to the self-guarding ego defenses my recent experiences had ushered. I faced the painfully familiar realization that my immediate family—my mom, dad, and sister—were on the other side of the country and I couldn't reach out to be supported and held by them. Even more so, I saw the implications of having run so far away from them in an effort to be independent and how alone this had made me, and how I was torn between living the life I wanted in the place that socially nourished me and my career without my family, and living a life close to my family without the social and entrepreneurial nourishment upon which I thrived. This brought the realization that I was without family or a partner to love and thus without the opportunity to create a new family through a child, which I one day wish to explore. I progressed from experiencing physical and emotional distance from friends and family to an incapacity to live out my primal mind's biological imperative of children, to which I hold a strong personal significance. Floating inside the tank, I opened up a byzantine can of worms that told me that I was an emotional failure of a human and would be utterly alone, forever.

Those realizations kept coming as I descended into deeper roots of pain, and with an increasingly potent emotional charge, my agony intensified. From the recognition of how alone I was to the unfolding awareness of what choices had led me to that point, the big picture was getting clearer as I progressed through the layers of memories. In the psychedelic lessons on my history of creating loneliness, a powerful memory came to mind.

When I was eighteen, I chose to break up with the greatest love of my life at that time, even though I was still in love with her. I felt like our relationship wasn't working because of some issues that wouldn't be solved in either of us unless we broke up on the grounds that we would never get back together. To do this, I believed I had to make sure she had the perception that we weren't getting back together. And so I repeatedly blocked out how devastated I was over our separation in order to look her in the face and tell her that I didn't love her even though it was a lie, because that was what I felt we both needed.

In hindsight, I can see how much this choice opened doors in my life that I don't regret opening and created a space for both of us to address the very issues we needed to in order to progress as young immature humans, but I also massively broke her heart. Floating in the tank, my body constricting, I was held accountable for those painful emotions, hers and mine, through reliving them all at once. But it was not just those emotions, it was the consequences of them as well. Finding clarity through the daedal perdition of this experience, I saw how I had guarded myself from repeating the grand consequences of love ever since then. I was fully aware of how this pattern of guarding, exacerbated by that experience in life but sourced in something even deeper, was playing out immediately in the current disconnection from my friends and my romantic partner, historically in my running away from home and the love of my family, and indefinitely into my future. Laid out in front of me was the entire web of choices that had severed me from all sense of grounded love, and I was experiencing the culminated emotional charge of all of it at once, seeing myself as an emotional pariah that was obviously going to die having forsaken himself of love. It was excruciating; I had never felt so alone, broken, and emotionally diseased.

Yet, somehow, even in the midst of all this pain, there was still a platform of awareness that allowed me to meta-navigate the situation. I have a lot of experience in dealing with shadow emotions on psilocybin, and in that experience, I know that part of the beneficial elements of facing the shadow is the catharsis, the emotional release that comes with it. And so in the midst of all this turmoil, I actively tried for it but I couldn't—there was no catharsis. There was only an increasing swell of energetic pressure in my chest correlating with an increasingly agonizing emotional charge. I wanted to cry or to scream, or something, anything, but nothing—just more swell.

The pressure in my chest and in my mind got so intense within the experience of loneliness, severance from love, and alienation that another one of my tools for navigating the psychedelic experience came up: *surrender*. It was as if the complexity and potency of those emotions got so strong, without any sense of catharsis, that the only thing I could do was just give in.

Ok! I get it, I'm alone. OK!

And then release, but no catharsis. I hadn't processed, let go, or addressed the implications of these emotions, I just accepted them and there was a sense of having released the pressure of resistance. I still felt like shit, though there was a noticeable ebb in my pain. It wasn't long, however, before that relative sense of release was realized as having only hit a checkpoint on my progression down the river of trauma. I simply handled the waters long enough to hit a smooth patch. The ride wasn't over in any way.

Being in the float tank is strange. Awareness moves in waves, transitioning from different levels of body awareness to dream-like visionary states and back to body awareness. After this moment of painful crescendo, I was back in my body, simply floating in the tank. There was a short set of moments where I took notice of my physical position in this space: partially submerged in water, floating on my back, tense but relatively relaxed, enclosed, the waves rolling on.

Further down the rabbit hole of self-exploration, new elements of emotional challenge emerged. However, they weren't exactly 'new' so much as they were the next layer of the trauma through which I had already begun moving. It wasn't a new set of emotions, but the next developmental stage, the next layer of depth from which my surface-level depression was precipitating. The pressure in my chest immediately returned to meet the same level as with the experience of exploring loneliness and disconnect, this time manifesting as regret and guilt.

Again, the pain was excruciating. I came to recognize my responsibility and fault in creating contexts in life that were inviting and perpetuating emotional pain in myself and in others. I began to clench my fists and my jaw tightly as the line of logic and memories dug deeper and deeper and things were made very clear to me. *I* was the one who chose to create all the heartbreak, to deny my love, to leave my family home and go so far away, to guard myself from the very thing that I needed to feel nourished. *I* was the person who had created the actions that generated the feelings of loneliness in myself and in my family who missed me, the one who chose to stay away from them for my own self-gain. *I* was the one responsible for the walls that blocked me from cultivating love and connection with others. It had been my choices that led me to hurt myself, physically and emotionally. I was the one setting myself up for all of this, and furthermore, I was responsible for the pain the consequences of those choices caused in the people I loved but was guarded from. I was responsible; I was at fault for all of this.

The potency of guilt and regret that came with this realization was indescribably strong. My whole body was writhing as if I were dying from some colony of flesh-eating insects that had invaded my chest and were eating my soul from the inside out. But still, no catharsis. Only pain.

"Why the fuck am I still in this goddamned tank?" I asked myself as if only for personal reassurance that in some strange masochistic way, I wanted this. I stayed with it.

What comes up in a mushroom experience, positive or negative, is emotionally honest. Regardless of what those emotions are associated to or what level of illusory attachment they may maintain, the emotions are honest. In their honesty, one is given the opportunity to hold themselves accountable and responsible for the effects those emotions hold within themselves. In doing so, one can integrate the subconscious implications these charged emotions have on one's personality. I call this *emotive-psychosynthesis*, and in my experience, it seems to only be functional if it comes with some sense of catharsis, a sense I had yet to experience at this point in my float.

And so I stayed in the tank, even to the point where I felt as though I may not have come back from it. The mammoth amount of guilt and regret building inside of me and the pressure I held in my body was tremendous. I felt as though I was about to completely break; my body would shut down and I would die of a self-broken heart in a dark watery grave, and then with a crumbled voice of humility...

Fuck it, ok, I get it... It's all my fault. I accept.

And then, release. A breath in, a breath out; but I wasn't finished yet.

Round 3: Hunting The Shadow

Over the past few years, I have developed a systematic approach, a framework to working with the mushroom for personal healing. Within this framework are what I call the four archetypes of psilocybin: *Surrender, Facing The Shadow, Uncovering The True Self,* and *Oneness.* * These archetypes are not independent

---

* You can find a fuller description of these archetypes in my other book *Decomposing The Shadow* (2013), or an audiobook called *The 4 Archetypes Of Psilocybin* (2014).

of each other in any way, but overlap within the experience, working more like recognizable themes than specific sections or segments. Additionally, within this framework is a discussion on how these archetypes unfold through creative visions and metaphors founded on a personally meaningful symbolism. A great example of this is what came next in the tank.

I had been floating in there for an eternity. My body was simultaneously very relaxed and deeply sore. I had gone through some of the worst emotional pain I could remember and more, all at once. Each progressing sequence of associated thoughts dug deeper into the layers of trauma I had inoculated in my psyche throughout the course my life. All of this was emerging as a consequence of me consciously choosing to take psilocybin mushrooms and enter a sensory isolation float tank to *face the shadow*, to face an inner honesty I had been subconsciously protecting myself from dealing with as a result of egoic defense mechanisms employed in childhood and developed throughout life. I entered the tank with an intention to face and release the potent energy of whatever darkness was being blocked by these psychological mechanisms of the ego. I entered this tank to address my current illness, the deep depression I was being overtaken by. I entered for *emotive-psychosynthesis*, catharsis, for healing. Yet so far, all I had experienced was a total excavation of my sense of emotional security, without the slightest sense of healing or benefit.

I no longer wanted to get out of the tank; I had given up trying to get away from the *true self*, the emotional honesty I was being exposed to. There was an end to this, and I needed to see it through. That is why I was in the tank, and I wasn't going to leave until I got there.

As I lay back in body awareness, sore from the physical expression of emotional tempestuousness, I caught a glimpse of something. This may sound weird, but while I was in a darkness so full that one would need to check to confirm whether their eyes were open or closed, I saw something move. I immediately knew that the emotional processes I was facing in the tank were being creatively rendered by my mind as a darkness moving across my field of vision. I had asked to be shown *the shadow* so that I could face it, and now there it was. My subconscious mind had worked with the mushroom to compile a metaphorical platform for pulling my conscious awareness to the source of trauma I sought through this visual hallucination. This access only came after I fully surrendered to my situation, and now that I had come this far, my ego tenderized and supple, I was ready to engage.

> *There is the shadow I was looking for.*
> *Hey you, show yourself to me!*
> *I am ready.*

Again, I had no idea how deep I needed to go, but I knew I hadn't gone deep enough. When I caught the glimpse of this 'shadow' moving past my eyes, it was clear that I was on the right track to further navigating my trauma, and the moment I called out to it, I was on the express route straight to its center.

Upon calling out the shadow, I was struck with a foreboding sense of peril as "be careful what you wish for" echoed through me in dissonant chords. The attention I placed upon this visual rendering of emotion immediately began to lead me through the amorphous terrain of my psyche. I could feel it redirecting my awareness from my floating body and into a fully engaged visionary experience. It came on quickly, but there was a moment about halfway between the worlds when something very important came to light. Intermittently since being a teenager, and consistently in the few months leading up to this experience, I had been actively meditating on a (mostly) daily basis. The intention of this was to increase my mental-emotional stability to more readily access an optimal state of performance in my creative and business projects. Apart from the blunt catalyzing of my recent depression, this had been working quite well for me. But at this halfway point, with a sense of peril pervading my emotional acuity, I understood that all of my meditation had been focused towards ego-driven goals: success, performance, efficiency, and so on. None of it had been cultivating what was really going to be useful in that moment, a reliable relationship to an unseen dimension of loving acceptance and support, God...

***

This word "God" throws people sometimes and I can understand why. Personally, I relate to it under the premise that the word "God" is a means to objectify an internal experience in order to build a relationship to that element of one's self. I understand this element of *self* as the source of all existence dynamically manifesting within the human experience. In its totality (though only existing experientially and beyond the capacity of human concepts to fully recapitulate it), it manifests as a *meaningfulness* that could be described as an unconditional, all-encompassing, unrelenting Love; in its divided attributes, it manifests in countless ways, including that of suffering. Using the cultural dialects available at the time, religious and spiritual traditions have created vast conceptual systems for implanting an ongoing relationship to this essence of one's self with varying degrees of complexity, legitimacy, and efficacy.

Why? One reason might be because if we cultivate a 'relationship to God' as representative of an unseen force of unconditional love held in high regards within ourselves, the active participation in that relationship may create an ongoing effect on self-identity. If done without the ego constructs of judgment and exclusion (all too popular in most conventional religious and spiritual institutions), we may be able to integrate some of the *meaningfulness* of unconditional love into life as a prevailing theme. We can keep that *meaningfulness* at the foundation of the often existentially insufferable experience of humanness. The appearance of the conceptual systems and psychological constructs played out in order to build that *meaningfulness* doesn't really matter, as long as they are reliably functional when needed, such as in times of suffering.

As far as I can tell, everything built inside of my mind, regardless of how prolific it interweaves into cultural consensus, is still an expression of the human mind wrapped in an illusory attempt at making sense of something beyond human capacity for understanding. This goes for everyone else as well. I don't see this as making the attempts towards understanding the nature of life as futile, but I do see it as an avenue to allow clausal disconnection from belief systems in order to more effectively build, navigate, and integrate our experiences and evade unnecessary conflict with each other. We create psychological constructs, belief systems, to make sense of this wildly novel *thing* we are all, to varying degrees, experiencing it as being 'self-aware of being alive.' Some of these belief constructs limit the scope of potential we have; others expand it. These constructs enable us to engage the most immediately available sense of life and 'reality' we have, while at the same time they are all merely psychological constructs we have built for ourselves or have allowed others to build for us.

Having this awareness allows us to be the architects of these constructs according to what does and does not work for each of us. With that being said, I believe that these constructs may fall into a spectrum of 'closer' or 'further away' from *truth* as an expression of being accurate facilitators to what is *real*, the all-encompassing 'something' existing experientially and beyond the capacity of human concepts to recapitulate it. In turn, some ancient and modern traditions or constructs (such as the teachings of the great mystical prophets, perhaps) may be closer to an expression of *truth* than others, potentially perceivable according to their universality, applicability, functionality, and how well they integrate the updated and continuously evolving human knowledge base.

The same concept of constructing belief systems to cultivate relationships to God can be applied in cultivating relationships to whatever other element of the *self* one chooses, such as the novel mindscapes of altered states. As a person who chooses to explore non-ordinary states of consciousness, and has often been dissatisfied with many of the available constructs for navigating those experiences, I choose to integrate what works for me and release what doesn't, claiming my place as the author(ity) of my own mind. One of the constructs that has worked for me in the past is similar to what anthropologist Michael Harner calls 'cross-cultural shamanism,' the foundational elements of 'shamanism' in general and across various cultures, explored in his book *Way Of The Shaman* (1980). The premise of cross-cultural shamanism as I have interpreted it is that of intentionally entering a non-ordinary state of consciousness, consciously navigating the subconsciously constructed dreamlike environment one enters, and investigating the symbolism represented within those metaphorical mind-environments.

I hesitate to integrate a complete identification with the system of cross-cultural shamanism, but some of it has continued to remain relevant and applicable to me throughout my journeys in life. One aspect is the ability to create a psychological representation of myself (like an avatar) to navigate an environment constructed by my subconscious mind, wherein every element of that environment is symbolically representative of different elements of my subconscious, even as deep as the aspects of me that connect to the transpersonal psyche, or the *collective unconscious* as Carl Jung calls it. Other elements I have found constructive for me are that of the power animal and spirit guides as psychological constructs representing different archetypal expressions of subconscious and transpersonal knowledge and wisdom, which can work as the means to feed this information back to my conscious mind. These 'guide' constructs can also play meaningful roles within my non-ordinary experiences, creating the ability to offer trust to an objectified element of myself to play a role my ego is resistant to or defensive of, thus taking the psychological load of needing to play that role off of my conscious mind.

As an example of how this may apply, at the time of my life that this story took place, I believed that building a relationship with my 'spirit guides' allowed me to confidently trust that 'they' would protect me in spiritual journeys through the turbulent realms of my mind. In hindsight, I have come to realize that this process of creating these types of constructs in my mind to help with psychedelic experiences is deeply sourced in the ego hijacking spiritual experiences to ensure its importance within them by creating an imaginative world of conflict and excitement where it is readily employed at all times. However, they also work as a personal mythos to align the subconscious with in order to better navigate and integrate novel emotional experiences or transformations. Like the premise of constructs around God being able to bring us closer or further away from what is *real*, these personally mythic constructs surrounding various elements of the mind can do the same depending on how we engage them.

These mythic/shamanic constructs aren't really necessary, nor are the manifestations of symbolism representing them inherently *real*. Yet in certain situations, having these types of constructs and the metaphorical contexts supporting them may potentially be functional and valuable tools for processing the information contained within the subconscious mind. Either way, this is where we get back to me in the tank, as I began to navigate my shamanic avatar deep into the fierce potentials of my mind.

***

I realized that I was about to enter a powerfully dark, emotionally turbulent realm of my subconscious and I hadn't taken the time to build the relationship necessary to feel that sense of trust in being protected. I felt alone and unsupported. This feeling wouldn't have arisen if I had been making a more conscious effort to build a relationship with the unseen dimension of loving support (God) that is always available, existing within and without me.

I recognized very quickly that I didn't feel confident in entering the darkness that was quickly consuming my reality and that I also felt disconnected from God, unable to call upon that support. So instead, I called up upon my spirit guides as the intermediaries between myself and this unseen dimension. Immediately, all the archetypal representations of the psychological constructs I had established in my mind as supportive figures for navigating challenging non-ordinary experiences came to me: a warrior, a sage, and a rabbit. I apologized for not choosing to actively participate in the awareness of unconditional support they helped me maintain. In response, I was very quickly offered the sense of loving acceptance and support I needed to believe in my ability to face what was about to unfold, but also that I needed to face it alone. 'They' only returned to enable my ego mind of duality to feel secure and know that 'they' were not needed, as I was the fullest expression of God in every moment, and in my fear I had simply forgotten that. 'They' also offered me a tool for navigating what came next: a reminder of *ho'oponopono*.

Ho'oponopono, as I have learned it, is a Hawaiian prayer that essentially goes "I'm sorry. I love you. Please forgive me. Thank you." It works on the premise that whatever comes up in life, regardless of what it is, we have played a role in creating it. In this creation role, there is a responsibility. Within this responsibility is the opportunity to humble ourselves and apologize for the manifest suffering. Whether this suffering is in ourselves or in another does not matter, as all of reality is mediated through the *self* as the creative principle behind all that is perceivable in the experience of *now*. Once we have apologized, we state the underlying essence of love that threads us all together. In love we do many things, beneficial and detrimental, but in essence, it is bred of love. From recognizing responsibility and apologizing, to sharing the foundation of loving awareness that can lead us to healing, we ask for forgiveness so as to let go and move forward, released of suffering. In asking, we can receive and express gratitude for that forgiveness and the release of suffering. "I'm sorry. I love you. Please forgive me. Thank you." Often this is done for one's personal issues, but can be expressed outwards onto anything in order to re-establish peace in the underlying psychological relationship we hold with that 'thing.' This prayer has helped me many times in life, and was about to be the means through which I faced some of the heaviest emotions I have ever engaged.

Round 4: Embracing The Shadow

With *ho'oponopono*, a sense of other-dimensional support and confidence in a valuable realization about cultivating a relationship to God, I non-physically stepped forth into the terror filling my entire torso. Immediately, I was ages away from my floating body and stood amongst grassy fields. The landscape in front of my *eyes*, was an enormous series of rolling hills, similar to the foothills of the Rocky Mountains combined with a fairytale meadow, rendered beyond normal resolution and in hyper-surrealist colours.*

My point of perspective was that of simultaneously being first-person and third-person; I was both standing on the ground looking out and looking at myself standing upon the ground. Framed in the third-person perspective, my (non-physical) body stood in the close foreground, positioned at the base of this mental scene. The mid-ground was that of the rolling hills coming to the horizon less than halfway up the vertical axis of my field of vision. As if mildly distorted, like a fisheye camera lens, the rest of my vision was that of a great and powerful sky filled with an incredibly foreboding storm. The stark contrast of the pleasant fairytale meadow composed of grassy hills and the wroth atmosphere above it was exquisitely harrowing. Like witnessing "the nothing" from the movie *The Neverending Story* pulling apart the lands, I saw this torrential storm in all its aggressive splendour pulling apart the soft honesty of the gentle rolling hills.

The cool, dark hues of purple, blue, and grey, washing like watercolour paints, were fading into black at the center of this massive, cyclonic storm cell. There was a line of some sort that was spinning down from its center to a point far off in the distance, just over the horizon and beyond a soft hill. I knew, in a knowing beyond the rational, that where the line met the earth was where I would meet the shadow.

With the intention of moving towards the point where the storm touched down, I transcended time and space and was spontaneously miles closer. This shift in location was immediate, but somehow there was still awareness of an anxiety congruent with having approached this epic scene slowly in real-time. The culminated emotional weight of this anxiety seemed to impulsively emerge upon me as spontaneously as my arriving

---

* I say *eyes* only as the best description of what I was 'seeing,' though my physical eyes were taking in no external light.

proximity. Standing atop a hill, looking down upon the apex of this tempest, I was offered my first look into the horrors I needed to enter.

The scene was reminiscent of *Star Wars: The Empire Strikes Back*, where Luke and Vader battle in the cloud city upon a narrow platform extending out into the centre of some massive machine. From my vantage point atop the hill, I could see a similar narrow platform extending out into the center of a large, infinitely deep, machinelike sinkhole in the earth. I couldn't see details very well. I was still a long range away and it was like trying to look through a typhoon. I could just barely make out in the midst of the massive, miles-wide storm above me, that along the platform there was a destination point. I had no ability to see what was going to be there, but I again felt a strong inner knowing that it was where I needed to go.

I was immediately even closer, with a sense of real-time continuity but no memories of movement to justify it. Standing at the outset of the platform, I felt the intense vertigo of leaning over the edge of the world. I walked with as much confidence as I could muster, though most of it was feigned at best, out towards the still hazy acme of this visionary experience. All my emotions intact, all my fear amplified, I once again transcended time and space and found myself at the last place I had expected to arrive...

I was back in the float room, but not in the tank. I was standing next to the tank with the room door on my right and the tank on my left. The size of the room was a bit exaggerated and it felt much larger than it actually was. There was a distinct multi-dimensional awareness in me, as I could feel myself still floating in the tank while also feeling myself standing next to the tank, knowing that I was next to myself who was in the tank as well.

The sense of terror I had been facing throughout this journey quelled slightly, but with the distinct sense of having hit the eerie calm at the eye of the storm. I knew that in the normally small, but now quite large area of the room where the chair and table resided in the alcove beyond my field of vision, was what I had come all that way to see. In that knowing, there was a deep sense of foreboding blended seamlessly with a gusto to hold my own and face that which was so deeply guarded in my psyche.

Taking a breath experienced in both my mind-travelling avatar awareness and my physical body in the tank, I took my first steps forward. It was like one of those dramatic film scenes where the camera pans in slow motion around the corner and you see that which was before only the 'terrifying unknown' slowly emerge as a concrete 'thing' that is far more disturbing than the 'unknown' it replaces. My vision slowly panned to the right and my anxiety crested as I took full sight of my archetypal shadow creatively rendered by the mushroom-enhanced subconscious mind. It was me; but not just 'me.' It was a frail, sick, decrepit, pale, broken, contorted, diseased me. Its skin was translucent, entirely covered by varicose veins and tightly wrapped around what seemed like a mere skeleton. Naked, crippled and lying sprawled on the floor like one would imagine a mentally ill leper would look like if they were found in the basement of some medieval asylum. We made eye contact as this diseased me used every ounce of its failing strength to communicate "Help, please."

I was immediately warped in my emotions; I was back in

the storm. This *me* that I saw there was some vital part of myself that needed help and I hadn't been giving it what it needed. This element of myself was the tender, vulnerable aspects of my psyche that I had been evading. In doing so I had locked it up in the deep dungeons of my subconscious for years and years. It was crying out to me for support and nourishment, and I was the only person who could help. Furthermore, I was responsible for the anguish and suffering it was experiencing. Nearly frozen in place by the obtuse horror and guilt churning up in me, I did what I knew I needed to do and went over to it, picked it up and cradled it into my arms. Holding this *me* and rocking it back and forth, I repeated "I'm sorry, I love you" over and over again as I began to feel in honesty the culminated emotional charge of every experience in life that further exacerbated the lonely suffering of this aspect of myself. Here was the catharsis I had yet to obtain. I began to cry.

Holding this frail, decrepit *me* in my arms and crying, I was re-experiencing all the pain I had seasoned at each different layer of traumatic memories and the realizations I had progressed through to get there. Furthermore, in some strange multidimensional awareness, I was also holding each of those memories expressed as a different *me*, as well as the psychical 'me' hurting in the tank, all at once. I experienced their pain culminated on top of my own as it all manifested in my floating body, and I cried. All at once, I cried through my body in the tank and through every *me* that I was simultaneously holding accountability for. With every inch of my entire being stretching out into the vast psychedelic darkness of the tank and the mindscape of multileveled emotional awareness, through the sobs, the choking and the tears, over and over again, I cried out:

I'm sorry, I love you. I'm sorry, I love you. I'm sorry, I'm sorry, I'm sorry...

117

Quantitatively, this went on for probably about twenty minutes or so. But qualitatively, it was an infinity of taking responsibility and holding emotional accountability for masses upon masses of unaddressed, unnourished suffering. Loneliness, disconnection, guilt, shame, inadequacy, regret—all of these emotions woven together at a depth of potency and complexity that is beyond words. The catharsis I experienced in those moments was among the most intense emotional purges I have ever felt, and I have been to some very deep, dark psychedelic spaces in my journeys with the mushroom.

Like when one has a really deep, full cry—where awareness shifts between being completely in the cry and also being just outside of it as if looking down on one's self and thinking "Wow, I'm really crying super hard"—I had a type of meta-awareness that came and went. In those brief moments of clarity, a few things became obvious. The first was fear of judgment, that somehow Skye, who was upstairs, would hear me or someone else would and judge me or worry that I was not okay and come check up on me, exposing my vulnerable experience to the air and out into the unsafe world. But I had to just let that go, because being honestly present with myself in my need for support superseded the need to be seen as strong and 'okay' and I understood that this was a very important lesson to hold moving forward with my life.

The other obvious realization that came in those moments of clarity was that I needed to complete *ho'oponopono* in order to fully process this experience. I knew that the next step was asking for forgiveness, but I was afraid to. I was worried that either I wouldn't be able to forgive, or I wouldn't understand how, or worse, that I wouldn't want to for some reason. This fear of asking for forgiveness, like all the other layers I faced, came to a crescendo and I burst out explosively with an enormous cry.

Please forgive me.

I didn't entirely understand to whom I was asking or from whom I was going to receive, but I asked with my whole heart and soul. In that moment, I was offered a realization that changed my life. It was sourced in the concept of asking for forgiveness from God, deeply embedded in so many religious traditions, which then made so much sense to me. It isn't that we ask for forgiveness to have some other thing forgive us, but that we create the context wherein we can offer ourselves the experience of forgiveness, offering and receiving. If we do not ask, how can we expect to receive? This experience of forgiveness is something we can learn to cultivate within ourselves—a gift many of us have yet to open, but it is vital that we do. Moreover, once we learn this forgiveness within ourselves, we will be able to offer it to others as well, another gift many of us have yet to open.

In all this new perspective on forgiveness, I saw that this step in *ho'oponopono* does not need to come immediately upon asking for a sense of healing to come. I didn't need to feel the forgiveness I so desperately needed in that moment to feel resolved. I understood that simply having asked and trusted that it would come in time was enough, and the tears slowed, and the tears stopped. My pain ebbed and I fell into release and gratitude, so much gratitude. My body floating, soft but shaken, I knew in that moment, I was ready to leave the tank.

Integration

Getting out of the tank took some finesse. I allowed myself to stretch and move, position and reposition, before I opened the lid. With the lid open, I sat up in the tank cross-legged to allow my blood pressure to stabilize before I came to standing. Once out, I wrapped a towel around me, closed the lid, and headed to the shower. I kept a sense of emotional cleansing in mind as I rinsed the leftover epsom salt off my skin and out of my hair. Thanking the water running over me, I allowed the emotional residue of my experience in the tank to be symbolically washed away. At the same time, I created the vision of integrating that broken *me* as an expression of all the layers of pain I faced back into myself; the two of us merging into one being, connected at a non-dimensional point of center, expressed as a healed, confident me.

Dry and dressed, I was still feeling noticeably raw from my experiences in there. Normally, procedure at The Cove was that you simply closed the door to the float room and headed back upstairs. Skye took care of all the routine cleaning and preparations for the next float. That time, however, was potentially the last time I would ever float in that tank, and definitely the last time I would ever float at The Cove. After so many powerfully meaningful experiences in there, I wanted to offer it an expression of gratitude. Not because the tank outside of me had some level of consciousness as to my actions and intentions, but that the tank inside of me, the inner construction of 'the tank' that holds a personal *meaningfulness* deserved an expression of gratitude, cultivated through conscious gestures of appreciation. So I helped myself into their cleaning closet, went back into the float room, and cleaned it as completely as I was able. That tank had offered me so much; it was the least I could do to wash it down in honour of all the cleansing it had offered me.

Thank you.

Back upstairs, I spoke very little with Skye about what I went through but simply expressed its intensity and my appreciation. I let him know that the tank and room were cleaned and that I was going to head out right away. We said goodbye in an honest hug of brotherly connection, and I left.

The walk home through the park was beautiful, but not in a "Wow, this is all so beautiful" sort of way; I didn't really feel like I was fixed or that life was all that great. Yet, there was a sense of beauty in my honest tenderness that allowed the energetic malaise of gentle melancholy to be reflected back at me by my environment in a way that communicated "It's beautiful because it's honest."

There was a noticeable change in my well-being right away, though there was no definitive point wherein I could say that I felt better. It was through a gradual transition of integrating that experience with reflection over time that I was able to not only come to terms with the context of what sparked my depression, but even come to embrace it with loving self-acceptance. This change in my relationship to that context matched the core *meaningfulness* of the metaphorical embracing of my shadow in the tank.

Work with the mushroom awakened a state of consciousness that has allowed me to move through deep personal trauma effectively and efficiently. Sometimes these experiences offer the 'healing' I am looking for right away. Other times, like this one, it takes a long time. Even at the point of writing, reading, editing, and rereading this story (over and over), I am still coming to new dimensions of integration, as well as new dimensions of gratitude for all that I have been offered and have offered myself throughout the many journeys into the layers of darkness I have faced.

OUTRO

The process of writing out these three stories has offered me a lot of perspective on these journeys and on myself as a constantly changing being. The revisitation, exploration, and verbalization of these experiences so far after the fact has allowed a space for consolidating not only what those experiences offered me at the time, but the insights that have emerged since then.

For those who, from personal experience, starkly believe in the benevolent potential of psychedelics, it is common to misconstrue these potentials as somehow universal. Even worse, this misconstrued perspective is then touted evangelically: "Psychedelics are the way and the light." I, with humility, have not been free of such propositions during my development as a psychedelic person.

In the three stories you just read, you will find perspective gained over years of exploring not only the psychedelic experience, but also the implications it has offered my self-awareness and personal development. Most essentially, the conceptual foundation of what is offered here is bred more of reading psychology textbooks than books specifically on psychedelics.

Between the lines of the last two paragraphs, I am offering two specific points.

The first is that psychedelics are NOT miracle tools for transformation. They are extremely dose- and relationship-dependent in regards to their potential successfulness as such tools. Furthermore, even when they do facilitate positive changes, there is no guarantee that those changes will hold. In personal experience, it holds more consistent that most of what is learned slips away, only to be remembered later in life with a "duh, you already know this" epiphany, only then to be likely forgotten again. This isn't to offer a defeatist attitude to the potential of psychedelics, but to reinforce the awareness that these tools don't necessarily make the changes for you. They can help to make personal changes more efficiently, yet only to the extent in which the user knows how to harness said tools. My books, and this one in particular, aim to offer devices and suggestions on wielding psychedelics with more effectiveness and confidence. They are bred of extensive study and *lots* of error. This leads to my second point.

As much as reading books on psychedelics such as this one can be directly applicable to better understanding the nature of the psychedelic experience and navigating said experience, they are not the most effective in garnering an understanding of the 'how' and 'why' the 'what' emerges from the psyche. I personally believe that reading books on psychology, neuroscience, spirituality, linguistics, philosophy, mythology, etc. will offer a more solid reference point for triangulating one's psychedelics experiences to the effect of successful integration. From there, books on psychedelics work more as a point of specific interest, rather than the essentially relied upon foundation for understanding one's psychedelic experience. I keep this idea in mind when I write, hoping to engender reading experiences and concepts for the reader that merge the two sides of this (admittedly) generalized dichotomy I just inadvertently created.

I hope that in reading this book, these three stories offered you something beautiful, even if only in the experience of reading itself. To paraphrase the words of famous jazz musician Jimmy Smith into my own:

I hope you enjoyed reading this book half as much as I enjoyed writing it for you.

I say this because I learned a lot about myself and what my experiences have offered me, something for which I am extremely grateful.

Thank you.

ABOUT THE AUTHOR

James W. Jesso is a Canadian author and public educator who is dedicated to helping to engender regenerative, accessible, and public discourse on socially outcast and taboo subjects. Jesso is a writer for Disinfo, Reality Sandwich, and PsyPressUK, as well as host of the podcast ATTMind Radio, through which he has authored numerous articles, essays, and videos, as well as radio, podcast, and interviews for various other channels, digital and print media. As a public educator, he has toured across the world giving lectures and facilitating public discussions on a variety of subjects. Most recently, he has taught in Peru on plant-based psychotherapy while touring the jungle, studying and exploring the use of Ayahuasca as a spiritual tool.

Learn more about Jesso through his homepage at: www.jameswjesso.com

Other Books by James W. Jesso

Decomposing The Shadow: Lessons From The Psilocybin Mushroom (2013)
Soundscapes & Psychedelics (2014)

54836904R00095

Made in the USA
Charleston, SC
15 April 2016